Benjamin

A loving story about a family and their dog and
his lasting impact on the animal kingdom

Dedicated to all the Benjamins in the World

Malcolm N. Bernstein

Produced by:

FriesenPress
Suite 300 – 852 Fort Street
Victoria, BC, Canada V8W 1H8

www.friesenpress.com

Distributed to the trade by The Ingram Book Company

Table of Contents

Foreword

This book is in honour of our pup Benjamin and everything he represents: goodness, innocence, unconditional love, boundless energy, incredible intelligence.

We hope that his story will touch and inspire you, make you laugh, brighten up your day and your life.

And make you feel good, knowing that all proceeds from this book are going directly to Humane Societies, SPCA's, rescue centres and animal welfare organizations around the world.

Woof!

Malcolm, Helen and Benjamin 🐾

A Dream Come True

Unbeknownst to me, Helen went looking for a doggie for my 50th birthday. Dog lovers both of us, with a soft spot for mutts from the pound, Helen visited the Toronto Humane Society and the SPCA in Oakville, a Toronto suburb, as her work with Wellspring — a network of cancer support centres — took her out to their Oakville facility on occasion.

At one point, she got a call from the SPCA in Newmarket, north of Toronto. They had a stray who had been at the shelter for two weeks, was "not glamorous, but the most laid back dog we have ever seen."

Saturday May 6, 2000. A glorious, warm sunny day. Helen tells me about her search, just shy of my birthday May 10. I couldn't believe it. I was so excited I couldn't wait to get up to Newmarket.

Given the distance (Newmarket was about 25 kilometres north of our then home in the suburbs), and my propensity to drive too fast on occasion, Helen assured me they were holding the pooch for us sight unseen.

We headed up after breakfast. The scene at the shelter was overwhelming. Cars and people galore, and a fevered pitch of barking from the literally dozens of dogs in outdoor cages desperately trying to get your attention. It was pandemonium and heart wrenching.

They told us to walk straight down the length of the shelter, and our little boy would be in a cage right at the end, at the juncture of another row of cages running perpendicular to the one we were walking along, and right next to the exit to the vast fenced-in grounds.

I remember walking towards his cage as if it were yesterday — the noise, the chaos, the hot sun — and then, Benjamin!

There he was, lying facing the front of this cage, tail wagging — and not a peep. No barking, no jumping — just a gentle mid-size little boy, with very long fur and the most beautiful face and eyes. It was love at first sight.

We immediately took him out for a walk on the grounds. He was playful, gentle, and friendly. We sat down and at one point he very gently took my hand in his mouth. We were enthralled with him. We "reserved" him right away and agreed to come back the next day to finalize things as they needed to neuter him and complete all of the paperwork.

After breakfast at Cheryl's Centre Street Deli the next morning, we took Benjamin out again, made arrangements for him to be neutered, paid the nominal $15.00 fee, and arranged to pick him up Wednesday on my birthday.

We couldn't believe it. It was a great feeling.

Until one has loved an animal, a part of one's soul remains unawakened.
Anatole Franz

A Brief History

There isn't much we can share about Benjamin's history to that point, because there was really nothing the SPCA knew.

He was found running around Newmarket, and had been at the shelter for two weeks. He had no tags, and a thick shaggy coat down to here. He weighed thirty-seven pounds, six to eight pounds under his ideal body weight. He was un-neutered.

To this date, we despair what he went through before being found. And we marvel at how he came through his ordeal as loving and gentle as one can imagine.

Our new vet, Dr. Rob Watson at Eglinton Veterinary Clinic, was recommended by our friends Nina and Jeff. Bob estimated Benjamin's age at eighteen to twenty-four months. He — and countless people since then — remarked what a beautiful dog Benjamin was — the most incredible multi-coloured wavy coat — rust coloured with grey and black flecks, a grey beard, bright eyes, and perpetual smile. Bob said he was a mixed terrier, but had no idea what the mix was.

A number of people say he's an Australian cattle dog and a few ask if he is a Dingo! A number of people have said he looks like fawn; and many have remarked Benjamin looks like "the doggie from the movies" (*Lady and the Tramp*, among others).

It wasn't till two years later, when we moved into the city, that we saw several border terriers in our area and it became clear Benjamin is a border crossed with something <u>much</u> bigger! The "grissol and tan" coat, grey beard, grey ring on the tail, and off-the-charts energy are classic border terrier, but as for the rest, who knows!

One thing is for sure. Benjamin is unique. The number of people who stop us on the street and say "What a beautiful dog" or "What kind of dog is that?" or "He's gorgeous" or "What a sweet face" is really incredible.

A New Member of the Family

Wednesday, May 10, 2000. Another magnificent day. We leave work early and head up to Newmarket to pick up our little boy! The excitement is palpable.

Out he comes, prancing and wagging his tail. Papers in hand, with temporary leash, collar and tags on him, Benjamin jumps into the car — front seat no less!

We head off to Petsmart at a local box store mall.

He *pulls* us across the parking lot into the store, and up and down every aisle like a house on fire! Sniffing, exploring, playing with other doggies — and peeing on the store floor! Thankfully, the staff were great about that. We had no idea what to feed him and went with the house brand of kibble to start us off.

An hour later, laden down with food, toys and a bed, we were on our way — to a new home, neighbourhood and life — for all of us.

Given the brilliant sunshine and incredibly warm sunny day, we immediately went into the back yard. Fortunately, all of us on the same side of the street had refrained from putting up fences so we had a long stretch of lawn for playing.

It was clear that Benjamin had never seen a toy — the tennis ball was a source of wonder to him. But in no time, he was fetching, demonstrating profound athleticism catching the Frisbee, and sprinting around the extended yard with a "bagel" clenched in his teeth and Helen in hot pursuit.

Inside was more of the same — chasing around the main floor and up and down the stairs. We learned a few things right away: Benjamin was smart, fun loving and incredibly agile. He was impeccably well mannered and totally non-possessive. He was everything anyone could ask for in a pet.

We also learned very quickly that Benjamin had had some bad experiences. While perfectly house trained, and quite happy to make himself at home on the couch, he would fly off instantly if one of us went to sit down next to him. It took quite some time before he would stay put let alone cuddle up — invariably with his mummy.

The next morning, I took Benjamin for a run and there began a form of communication between us that Helen and I have continually found amazing. Benjamin would knock my knee with his nose to tell me what he wanted — be it to take a certain street, head in a particular direction, or knock and stare at the water bottle for a drink right now! Let alone for a cookie! (Benjamin is a cookie monster; thankfully he gets plenty of exercise, and burns everything off).

Our house backed onto a park, and bordered a walkway. In short order, our place became a drop-in centre for the doggies in the area on their way to and from the park. One winter Sunday morning, John and his big golden Cujo dropped by unannounced. Cujo and Benjamin were tearing up the house, snow and mud from Cujo's paws everywhere, up and down the stairs, barking and wrestling, until finally Cujo dove onto the bed where Helen was still asleep!

It took no time for Benjamin to become the "chief instigator" of play time in the park. He would tear out the door, down the walkway (there were no streets or cars to worry about) and into the park where he would promptly get a whole pack of neighbourhood pooches chasing him! His speed, athletic ability, instincts, and mischievousness are to this day truly incredible.

Were Benjamin a football player, he would be the greatest open field runner who ever lived!

If you're thinking about a pet, why not consider a stray or a pet given up for adoption? There are many shelters and rescue organizations to choose from. You would get an animal that would shower you with gratitude and unconditional love, and save a life in the process. (You'd also pay a lot less than a purebred!). It doesn't get any better.

If you have a few minutes, do some basic checking into food beforehand. Your new family member will be hungry! The pet stores are chock full of choices, and your new vet can also advise. (Yes, you will need a vet, too!)

I imagine all the products are good, admittedly organic may be better if within your budget. Find out from the shelter or breeder what they have been using.

You may anticipate that over an extended time, your pet's eating habits might change. For example, in Benjamin's case, we have changed his food several times, as his digestive system — and tolerance to certain foods — changed, from a "plain Jane" brand that we finally realized was devoid of nutrition and comprised in part of 'renderings' (aka contents of dubious origin!) to lamb-based kibble topped with a yummy carrot and peas baby food blend, to chicken based kibble, to, eventually, a prescribed canned food for sensitive tummies, topped up with a lot of homemade cooking, which I discuss later.

Oh, one more thing. Early on, when we got Benjamin, I was watching him eat from his bowl on the floor when one day it struck me that this was really unfair! Why does my pet have to eat standing up with his head at a 90 degree angle straight down? Quel horreur! It turns out we had a cheap plastic footstool from Canadian Tire, which Helen (being short) used to get things from the ridiculously high kitchen cupboards (or sometimes just to put her feet on at the kitchen table!). I appropriated it immediately and from then on it became Benjamin's.

Being a rather tall dog (for a terrier), it was perfect for him! He never had to eat or drink from a bowl on the floor again!

Since then, the pet industry has brought out designer bowls on fancy stands, but really, a good old-fashioned stool from your local hardware store is just fine if you don't want to splurge to that extent.

*Once last thing on the subject of food. **Remember:** Water on demand! Always have a bowl of water out if you have a dog and always carry water as soon as the weather gets even remotely warm. You can get a water bottle at any pet store. Don't leave home without it!*

Meeting our Families

Victoria Day weekend, 2000 provided us with our first opportunity to drive to Montreal with Benjamin for a visit with our families.

While he took instantly to being in the car for drives around town, it was clear that travelling long distances was a new experience. Benjamin actually stood the whole way to Montreal! He was very excited, but also exhausted by the experience. Of course, we stopped many times; and a five and a half hour trip has now become seven to eight hours. Still, we *hate* the thought of leaving Benjamin behind with anyone else (aside from Allison who has been a godsend over the years if we do take a week down south in the winter); and we would *never* put him in a crate on a plane.

Benjamin is a doggie's dog. He loves playing with anything that moves, has a wonderful disposition, is totally innocent and has no sense of danger. He is, however, very shy with strangers, but also has the most incredible calming effect on people. I recall one evening when we had our good friends Dave and Rita over. Rita is very fearful of dogs. Benjamin would not leave her side the whole night and, in the space of a few short hours helped her transcend her fear in a way one could only describe as miraculous. Benjamin had the same effect on my mother Elsie, who had a similar aversion to dogs. Helen's parents had always had dogs so there is a natural connection there. Likewise, with our sisters, Nancy, Louise and Diane, partners Roland and Keith, and my late cousin Sydney, all of whom are dog lovers.

Of all the family encounters, though, the first one with my late father Bob was something that will forever stay in my mind. I recall the moment as vividly as if it just happened. My dad, who had severe arthritis in his neck, was sitting up in bed and getting ready to join us in the front of the house. He was a dog lover and Benjamin sensed that love instantly. Benjamin walked into the bedroom towards the bed — something that was very surprising given his shyness — and just so effortlessly jumped on the bed and crouched down right next to my dad! Bob patted Benjamin's head and laughed. It was the most amazing sight I have ever seen. I truly believe there was a connection between the two of them that long predated that visit.

And Benjamin was the key to my being able to deal with my dad's passing later that summer.

Puppy School

Benjamin is very strong, and shortly after we got him, he gained some much needed weight and started to fill out nicely. He is muscular and sleek with a gorgeous coat. When he puts his head down and decides to chase after something — for example, if his mummy is joining up part way through a walk and Benjamin sees her a block away — he can almost pull me off his feet running towards her! Or when he takes my mitt in the middle of winter (!) and decides to run the length of the park off leash (or down several city blocks on leash), he is very hard to stop.

This is all good fun. It wasn't funny though, as shortly after we got him, he almost pulled us across Centre Street, a very wide thoroughfare near our home in Thornhill, when we were on our walk one evening and he saw a fox on the other side. We signed up for doggie training the next day.

Benjamin aced puppy school and went on to get his pet therapy designation. (We actually have not pursued that activity, as Benjamin is so energetic he would want to go to every nook and cranny of a facility but likely not want to sit at someone's side for any length of time). Nonetheless, when you pet Benjamin or give him a cookie (we carry tons of them), he always obliges with a kiss on the outstretched hand. This is a real thrill in particular for an elderly person. Whenever a child wants to pet him, he is as gentle as can be.

Pure Goodness

It was a beautiful Sunday afternoon in August during the first summer we had Benjamin.

We were on a short walk through a parkette a few streets away from the house when Benjamin — well trained by then and off leash — lay down in the grass. We learned very early on that Benjamin loved the sun — lying in the hot sun after a meal, or any time during the day is one of his favourite things to do (walking any distance in the heat, however, is unbearable for him).

But this was different. Benjamin was lying with front paws stretched straight out and his nose pointing straight ahead. I came over to check on him, and low and behold, there was a baby bird just a few inches away. Another pooch may have seen this poor little thing as a toy or prey, but not Benjamin. Benj wouldn't hurt a fly — literally. If another dog takes his toy or eats from his bowl, he isn't bothered at all.

Benjamin just lay in the grass watching over the little baby bird, waiting until we came over. At that point, with no one around and no nest in sight, we placed a series of calls, finally connecting with someone at the regional wildlife control centre. The advice was to leave the little bird; in all likelihood, it had fallen from a tree and its mother would come and get it. Touching it, let alone trying to put it back in its nest — if you could even find that — would lead to parental rejection.

With much regret, we carried on. When we checked the same spot that evening, the little bird was gone and we prayed that it was rescued by its mom.

Fast forward to 9 p.m. January 5, 2009. We were on our nightly walk with Benjamin in the bitter cold. All of a sudden, he stops and starts sniffing a grey-black object. It turns out to be a pigeon lying in the snow, undoubtedly injured. Benjamin was almost nuzzling its head — fortunately the pigeon didn't react! Benj was very reluctant to move from the spot, so we called animal control; the officer promised he would come by shortly, so we moved on.

We have had many such experiences with Benjamin — whether coming nose-to-nose with a fawn in the wilds of Mont Tremblant region in Quebec; or giving a frail elderly person a kiss on their outstretched hand to make their day. He is a very special little boy.

Researchers have noted that when children grow up in a home with a dog or cat they are less likely to develop allergies. Same is true for kids who live on a farm with large animals. In addition, higher levels of certain immune system chemicals indicate a stronger immune system activation, which will keep children healthy as they get older.

MedicineNet.com

Animals are incredibly intuitive. Their senses are far more acute than ours, and their natural tendencies to nurture, love, help, and protect other creatures and people is exceptional. We see news clips or read articles almost weekly about the lifesaving capabilities of dogs or their acts of courage and heroism.

Animals live in the moment. They possess an inordinate amount of playfulness, compassion, and native wisdom. We can learn so much from the animal kingdom, if we simply take the time to do so.

The Late Night Call

Anyone with a parent or family living in another city knows the fear a late night phone call instil instantly. August 27, 2000. The phone rings shortly after midnight. An emergency room doctor at the Jewish General Hospital in Montreal is on the line for me — my father had just been rushed there by ambulance. A short conversation ensues regarding emergency treatment and immediate intervention is agreed to. Just after midnight, the phone rings again. My dad had passed away.

Hanging up the phone, I sat down and was distraught. My father was a prince of a man and a best friend. Instantly, Benjamin jumped up on me — front paws on my knees, acute alarm in his face, tail wagging very fast. For that moment, comforting Benjamin became the focus for both Helen and me. And it helped tremendously.

After the phone calls, and then discussing travel options — me flying to Montreal on the first plane out and Helen driving with Benjamin, or all of us driving down in the morning, we opted for the latter. Upon arrival in Montreal, given the circumstances and space constraints, I stayed with my mother and Helen and Benjamin stayed at Helen's parents' home in another part of the city. Benjamin, typically a very relaxed little boy, was upset not knowing where I was and wouldn't eat. The second day in Montreal, Helen brought her parents and Benjamin to visit. It was great for everyone to be together. That night, Benjamin wolfed down his supper, content in the knowledge that *his* daddy was fine.

It only takes 15 to 30 minutes with a dog or cat or watching fish swim to feel less anxious and less stressed. Your body actually goes through physical changes in that length of time that makes a difference in your mood. The level of cortisol, a hormone associated with stress, is lowered. And the production of serotonin, an important chemical associated with well-being, is increased. Reducing stress saves your body a lot of wear and tear.

MedicineNet.com

The Big Move

April 2002. After 20 years living in the suburbs, and commuting to our jobs in the city in what was becoming unbearable traffic, Helen and I decided to sell our home and downsize to a condo in midtown Toronto. Even so, I was reluctant given the tranquility of our surroundings and especially the yard we all loved.

Beside the commuting, two things clinched the decision for me: Helen and I enjoyed living in downtown Montreal for several years prior to moving to Toronto, and she really missed city life; and, Helen would drop off Benjamin at doggy daycare every day on her way to work and one day he absolutely did not want to leave the car. We knew from that that he had outgrown the daycare setting and was really becoming bothered by all the puppies. It was time for a change. Moving into the city would free up countless wasted hours commuting. Moreover, the location we chose would also allow me to be at home a lot more, given that it was just a few blocks away from my office. So, Helen or I could walk Benjamin during the day quite readily.

Nonetheless, I was terribly worried about how Benjamin would fare with the move. I needn't have been!

We spent the first year in an apartment, waiting for the new condo building to be completed. Our interim digs was a one bedroom in a big sprawling sixties high rise — beautiful grounds, terrible tasting water, every conceivable cooking smell wafting through the vents! But, were there ever parks in the area! We discovered the incredible ravine system of Toronto where you can walk, run, and cross-country ski and not even feel like you are in the city. Benjamin had a ball that year, doggies everywhere, lots to see and do, the three of us "camping out" in close quarters. He adjusted to elevators and to the whole scene in no time!

Benjamin really came into his own in the city. Still very shy with people, he gradually became less so, and got more compliments about his beautiful looks and captivating personality than one can imagine. When we moved into our new home a year later, Benjamin adjusted to that in a nanosecond as well.

Considering the needs of your pet is a given when contemplating a move.

How will you get him or her to the new destination if a long haul? Are the new surroundings 'pet friendly'? Will you need to arrange for a pet sitter/walker if, for example, you are giving up a dog run with flapped door from the garage of your home to allow your pet to go in or out on their own during the day, and are now moving to an apartment or a condo? If a condo, are there restrictions as to type, size, or number of pets?

These are all basic considerations and will avoid any unnecessary surprises in what otherwise could be an enjoyable, albeit perhaps somewhat stressful, experience!

The "Joys" of Dog Ownership

Thursday, January 15, 2009. Minus 30 degrees Celsius with the wind chill.

Cold even for Benjamin, who loves the cold. Benjamin has a loose tummy on his mid-afternoon walk. We are immediately alarmed. He has had this before — which doggie hasn't? — but it is always concerning. You start going through a mental check list: What do we feed him? Did he eat some bark off a stick? Benjamin loves to pick up branches and run with them, and he always has trouble afterwards.

Helen made boiled chicken and chicken soup earlier in the afternoon — no spices, as wholesome as it gets, and one of all our favourite dishes — and she gave Benjamin a small portion over a bed of kibbles to help settle his tummy.

His tummy is fine on the late night walk and we are relieved (pardon the pun!).

We have had several other occasions, though, where Benjamin has had an upset tummy and wants to go out in the middle of the night — very often in the depths of the winter. He'll get up from his bed right next to ours, run to my bedside very animated — Benjamin knows who the light sleeper is — put his head under my immediately outstretched hand, and paw the bed as if to say "I need to go out right now!"

After a few nights of this in succession (not to mention the times when Benjamin just wants to go out in the middle of the night to chase his tail and play!), you can imagine the exhaustion. But I don't mind. If our little boy needs something, we're both there for him. He certainly is for us.

Short Order Cook

At one point, Benjamin's tummy problem lasted for an extended period of time. Through a process of elimination, (pardon the pun again!), and extensive consultation with Dr. Bob, we determined that his lamb-based kibble was too rich for him and he was having trouble digesting it. It took a month to slowly introduce a prescribed diet, which settles the stomach but wasn't intended to be a long term solution; and gradually integrate a chicken-based kibble which he seemed to really like.

While we have always topped up his kibble with baby food — chicken or beef and veggie, this last episode of tummy upset led us to look at a range of different solutions. After extensive consultations with Dr. Bob and his colleagues Drs. Chip Coombs, Jen Hodges, Paul Hodges and Bev Bateman, we gradually brought the amount of kibble down from ¾ cup to ½ cup twice a day; and began topping it routinely with homemade food, often prepared exclusively for Benjamin! Grilled salmon, baked chicken, beef or turkey burgers, spencer steak — much of these we don't even make for ourselves! — or scrambled eggs. And always steamed veggies — beans, broccoli, carrots, occasionally baked or sweet potato (not to mention raw carrots quite regularly during the day).

Since then, Benjamin has been so excited about his food! He starts licking his chops in anticipation of his meal the minute he gets home from the first outing of the day — a walk or run with me around five in the morning; and after his late afternoon walk with Helen. Come 5 p.m., Benjamin is standing in the kitchen licking his chops and whining if dinner isn't ready!

One of us — usually Helen — cooks for him, and then starts cooking for us! No wonder she refers to herself as a short order cook!

After Dinner Games

Benjamin loves to sleep after his meals — especially in the sun after his breakfast!

But after dinner, he first wants to play!

No sooner has he polished off his meal then he runs down to the closet where his toys are (if they aren't already strewn all over the house), swings opens the door with his nose or kicks at it if it's closed — and takes one toy out at a time, running down the hall, tossing it in the air and biting it till it squeaks. Then the next one — and so it goes, the after-dinner ritual and sheer exuberance, until one or all three of us is exhausted.

Benjamin then hits one of the couches for his power nap, all the while gearing up for his last walk of the day — this time usually a solid hour (freezing cold excepted).

Winter in the City

Benjamin is definitely a cold weather dog. While he craves the sun from early spring on, even with his summer haircut the heat knocks him out (me too!). A crisp cool to cold sunny day is his favourite weather, and boy does he love snow.

Salt, however, is a killer. Aside from being bad for the environment and animals, it is extremely painful for pets' paws. In Benjamin's case, being very active (and, like a true terrier, very stubborn when he wants to be! — he won't wear boots nor a coat, even in the rain which he absolutely *hates*), the salt is problematic.

Salt on sidewalks and roads is definitely the bane of our winter existence, as is ice and unplowed sidewalks — all of which are the norm in Toronto, a city that just can't get its act together when it comes to dealing with the realities of our harsh winters.

So, aside from Helen and I carrying a towel all winter to wipe the salt off Benjamin's paws, I will often pick Benjamin up and carry him for a block or more just to avoid the salt which some incredibly lazy home owners and apartment superintendents use instead of shovelling. It makes us really angry and there is very little you can do about it. People know they can simply get away with doing nothing to maintain their properties in a responsible manner from December to April.

We are grateful to the few who clear their sidewalks and use pet friendly de-icing products.

We often will drive to a large reservoir park in our area so that Benjamin can romp and frolic in winter in a salt-free environment. If you can get your pet accustomed to wearing boots from a young age, you're ahead of the game. As I mentioned, this was a non-starter in our case — although we could have probably opened a pet store with all the boots we have tried over the years! (eventually to the benefit of Toronto Humane Society as part of our occasional deliveries there).

On the Road

What once took us five to five and a half hours to drive to Montreal PB (pre-Benjamin) and weather permitting, became seven plus with all the 'Benjamin stops' along the way.

Benjamin doesn't particularly like travelling, so the stops are important. Fortunately, all the highway gas stations/restaurant facilities on Highway 401 have large picnic areas in summer so the stops are a pleasure ("trekking areas" in knee-deep snow in winter are fun *if* accessible, otherwise these stops are nightmares — almost *nowhere* to walk, ankle deep in slush and not fun!).

However, we soon realized that trying to make the trip in one day was too much, especially given our typical mid-day departure (once every conceivable last chore is done and all of Benjamin's goodies, bed, Frisbee, food and water supply are packed!).

So now we stop in Cornwall each time, one hour west of Montreal. The Best Western has a nice big property adjacent to a lovely quiet subdivision — great for an early morning summer run with Benjamin or a late night walk up to see all the lights and decorations at Christmas. We "camp out" in a big but very affordable room; they put in a microwave so that we can heat up Benji's baby food topping for his kibbles, and settle in for a movie after our last walk of the day.

On our trip down from Toronto, the next day it's on to the Sheraton Centre in downtown Montreal — the only hotel in the city we know of that allows pets — at least, without a huge surcharge.

Benjamin loves staying there. He sees his friends on the staff, loves riding the elevators and running down the hall to and from the room, and definitely loves romping on Mount Royal during the course of our stay.

He is a fun-loving little boy, likes any new (or repeat) adventure, and makes life on the road a fun experience.

If you are driving, put food and all pet-related items at the top of your travel checklist! Keep the food in a cool storage place while travelling. Make sure you chart a course with pet friendly accommodations, and book well in advance! Anticipate a longer trip because of stops, especially if you have an active pet. And always keep water in the car for stops.

If you are flying and planning to stow your pet in a crate in the cargo hold, I would urge you to think carefully about this. Aside from what must be a traumatic experience for your pet, there have been enough stories of pets that escape from their crate or are otherwise lost in transit to give one pause and perhaps reconsider this mode of transportation.

Summer Vacation

The Mont Tremblant area of the Laurentians is our favourite place. Helen and I used to downhill ski there and cross-country in the magnificent provincial park, where you can go for hours in deep snow through magnificent fir-treed forests, sheltered from the wind, and not see a soul!

From the second we turn off the access road that leads from Route 117 to the old village and start to drive up through the mountains to this secluded cottage we rent, Benjamin is up, tail wagging, and in a state of great anticipation. All windows are now open as we drive very slowly on this back road and Benjamin sticks his head out to take in the sights, smells, sounds and wind knowing that he will soon be at our destination.

The typical day starts with a run down a winding side road to the bike path — an incredible hard packed sand and crushed stone converted railroad line which goes for 200 km and used to carry the *P'tit Train du Nord* and its thousands of vacationers from the 1930s to the 60s. We head back from the path the same way, but this time it's much tougher! Of course I stop frequently for Benjamin to sniff and mark, and the steeper hills we walk — it is quite a climb! And then the reward: a short walk down a trail to a pristine lake for a dip while Benjamin romps along the shore, and another short walk from there to the cottage for a sumptuous breakfast. After that, none of us care what we do the rest of the day! It just doesn't get any better.

The most special part of the vacation is our nightly ritual — driving to the old village, and walking along the bike path the length of Lac Mercier where you see the most spectacular sunsets imaginable. But the highlight is what happens when we are about five minutes into our walk. Benjamin picks up his already fast pace and begins to trot toward a house just off the path, runs into the yard, and looks for his girlfriend Savannah, a short stocky yellow lab who leaps off the porch a very long flight of stairs up, bounds down to greet him, and, both tails wagging furiously, heads off with Benjamin in tow along the path for our nightly excursion! It puts a grin on our faces from ear to ear.

The same scene repeats itself every night we are there other than evenings with the occasional — and often quite violent — thunderstorm. The two pooches finish off with a ritual flat out race around a huge landscaped property near Savannah's home, a football field long and wide, Benjamin barking at Savannah to chase him with no hope of catching him — until they are completely exhausted. Needless to say, Benjamin is fast asleep in the car on the drive back to the cottage, which we do slowly to savour every minute *and* watch for wildlife on the pitch black road.

Malcolm's Health Bars — First Made at Tremblant
Benjamin's Favourite!

1 cup whole wheat flour
1 cup oat bran
¾ cup wheat germ
1 ½ cups skim milk powder
½ cup brown sugar
½ cup molasses
½ cup peanut butter
½ cup chopped pecans
½ cup chopped walnuts
½ cup chopped dates (or any other dried fruits you like)
2 eggs
¼ cup vegetable oil

1 tbsp. baking soda
2 tbsp. baking powder

Mix all dry ingredients in a large bowl and all liquid
ingredients in a separate bowl.

Blend the liquid ingredients with the dry mix.

Line a 14 x 9 inch Pyrex with two pieces of parchment paper placed perpendicular and coat the paper
with a dab of vegetable oil.

Pour the integrated mix into the Pyrex and bake at
400° F for 20-22 minutes.

Remove and let stand until the mix hardens with a
nice crumble crust!

Remember!

Never feed raisins, grapes, or chocolate to your dog,
and check with your vet about onions and garlic. And
always consult your vet if unsure about the contents of
any given food item.

A Sixth Sense

As you know by now, Benjamin is a very sensitive and intuitive pup.

March 12, 2009. We are on our late afternoon walk. Two blocks away, he comes to a full stop at an acquaintance Mary's low rise apartment building. Earlier that week, Mary lost her best friend Jenny, a sweet 16-year old little mix. There was no way that Benjamin would have known this, if thought about it from our (somewhat limited) human perspective.

But stop he did, right at the building, sat down and wouldn't budge. As it happens, a friend of Mary's was just leaving the building, and went inside to get her. Benjamin nestled against Mary and let her pat him — something he had never done before.

This, like everything else in this book, is a true story. Benjamin has a sixth sense, a sensitivity, and a way of knowing things that almost defies description.

We think all animals have this. They are sentient beings and know things intuitively. We can learn so much from them — if only we would let them teach us.

A "seizure dog" is one that has been specially trained to live and work with people who have epilepsy. Some are trained to bark and alert parents when a child is having a seizure outside or in another room. Some lie next to a person having a seizure to prevent injury. And some work is being done in training dogs to warn before a seizure occurs, which gives the person time to lie down or move away from a dangerous place such as a hot stove.

MedicineNet.com

Getting Serious for a Minute

Canada's animal protection laws had remained essentially unchanged for over one hundred years until 2011 when the government passed Bill C-10 Cruelty to Animals under the Canadian Bill of Rights provisions for property.

While representing progress in terms of fines, the most meaningful aspect of animal welfare — recognition of animals as *sentient beings* with intelligence and feelings — was overlooked despite the massive amount of supporting evidence, both anecdotal and scientific. Consequently, the legislation continues to refer to animals as "property", as an accommodation to the power of certain vested interests and even wealthy helicopter-hunters, who wouldn't know sportsmanship if their lives depended on it.

And yet, stories of the kindness and wisdom of animals are well documented — of dogs performing heroic acts to save people; serving as search and rescue team members in disasters; guiding the visually impaired; adopting troops in war zones; staying by their master's side for days after he has been ambushed or slain; volunteering in hospitals and nursing homes.

In *The Age of Empathy* by Dr. Frans de Waal, we read about a female elephant that acted as a guide for a blind but unrelated female. On CBS News, we see the story of Tara, an elephant at the Elephant Sanctuary in Tennessee, and her best buddy Bella, a stray mutt she adopted on the sanctuary grounds. The two have been inseparable since they met. When Bella suffered a spinal cord injury and was in the sanctuary hospital for three weeks, Tara maintained a vigil outside the building virtually without moving until Bella recovered, and trumpeted in happiness and jubilation the day Bella was carried out on the balcony for Tara to see.

We see the incredible story of Jasmine, an abandoned, emaciated and abused Greyhound adopted by the Wildlife Sanctuary in Nuneaton Warwickshire, England, who, after regaining her health, in turn adopted fox cubs, badger cubs, chicks, guinea pigs, stray puppies, rabbits and a Roe deer fawn, comforted them, and made them part of her new "family".

We are gratified when we read the accounts of immense courage by people who rescue animals in distress — in New Orleans after Hurricane Katrina; in Los Angeles on January 22, 2010, when a helicopter firefighter team rescued a stranded dog in the Los Angeles River after torrential rains; in Thailand where families adopt elephants whose natural habitat has been destroyed. We read about the people of McBride, British Columbia, who dug a two mile path through a good 10 feet of snow to rescue abandoned horses in December 2009. And we see TV documentaries of hard core prisoners participating in animal rescue programs, training wild horses in Colorado and giving both man and four-legged creature a new lease on life.

And then, there are the horrible acts of animal cruelty — by sadists who injure and kill animals; by people who perpetuate dog fighting rings; by fishing fleets which slaughter dolphins and whales en masse in complete contravention of international treaties; by hunters who hire a helicopter to shoot their big game trophy; by abattoirs that kill beautiful, sensitive wild horses or race horses which are past their prime; by poachers who kill elephants, tigers and rhinoceros for their tusks, skins, or some perverse superstitious belief in the healing power of some of their body parts.

And there are animal husbandry practices we have legitimized, such as force-feeding chickens 24/7, raising hogs in severely overcrowded conditions, farming fish in over-medicated lice-ridden ponds, all to maintain our standard of living and quality of life, so called.

Let's tackle this once and for all and work toward getting substantive animals rights legislation passed in this country. Legislation with integrity. Let's take the effort global. Through education, cooperation, cajoling and/or threatening with our votes, let's join with many others and do our part to change the world for better.

And help us make The Benjamin Project a reality, by instilling in children around the world a love for animals, an understanding of the incredible intelligence and capacity for good these creatures possess, and an ability to discern right from wrong where animal welfare is involved.

Fact: 75% of young offenders have an early record of animal cruelty.

So Much Love

In 1870, when George Graham Vest coined the term "Man's Best Friend," was he ever right. The unconditional love and loyalty that emanates from our little boy is a perpetual wonder to both of us. If you get up and move to a different room, Benjamin is right there. When we had the house, you'd go up and down the stairs umpteen times a day, and he would accompany you every time.

Our greatest desire was to give Benjamin a good home, and try to make up for whatever hardships he experienced before he came into our lives. To shower him with affection, and give him a sense of security and wellbeing.

As one of our friends, Rhona, who knew Benjamin as a very shy new member of our family, remarked a few years later "He's got so much self-esteem!"

Benjamin has been a limitless source of joy since the day we got him. He only wants to please and play, is very sensitive to your moods and situation, and is a friend to any other two or four-legged creature.

He is the best little pup in the whole world.

Aren't they all?

Benjamin 🐾

GOING FOR DADDY'S CAP, Photo by David Shaul

LOOK AT ME! Photo by David Shaul

CATCH ME IF YOU CAN! Photo by David Shaul

READY TO CHASE, Photo by David Shaul

LOOKING BACK AT DADDY, Photo by David Shaul

KNOWING LOOK, Photo by David Shaul

KING BENJAMIN!

HAVING A COOL ONE

PLAYING WITH SAVANNAH

AT THE LAKE

CHILLING WITH DADDY

FAST ASLEEP

Benjamin 🐾

GAZING AT MUMMY

WAITING FOR DINNER

43

DINNER IS SERVED

WATCHING DUCKS

A BIG YAWN!

CUDDLING WITH MUMMY

BLISS

HANDSOME BOY

Two Years Later

The third week of June 2012. Benjamin is experiencing another of his gastrointestinal disorders characterized by diarrhea and many urgent middle-of-the-night outings. Mixing steamed rice with his food wasn't helping, nor did a round of antibiotics. Moreover, his pees, especially the first one or two immediately upon getting outside, were unusually long.

It didn't help that, during this time, I had a lower back problem brought on by cleaning out the locker! Walking, bending down to tie my running shoe laces, any slight turn was excruciating — and my shrieks really spooked my sensitive little boy. Fortunately, a visit to our family doctor and a couple of anti-inflammatories later, and the pain was gone. But our real problem was just starting.

June 27. On the way back from a quite long 6 a.m. walk, about three blocks from home, Benjamin circled twice very quickly and fell over fully stretched out on his left side. I was in a state of panic. I ran to the house whose property we were in front of and pounded on the door to ask for help, a lift … no answer. Someone came by and I cried out, "*I need help!*" not knowing what she could even do for us. And then, cradling Benjamin in my arms, wrought with emotion, I carried him home, rode up the elevator with the concierge who opened the door to our unit, and put Benjamin inside — at which point he stood straight up, shook himself and wagged his tail! I was overcome with joy, but also with concern.

I immediately called and left a message for our vet, and we headed over upon opening at 8 a.m. Of course, Benjamin was in fine form! Dr. Bob checked him out, and all vital signs were A-okay! The only conclusion Bob could reach, quite legitimately at the time, was a case of idiopathic vestibular syndrome — that is, an occurrence of no known origin. To be on the safe side, Bob referred us to a classmate of his, Dr. Sue Cochrane, a neurologist at Veterinary Emergency Clinic (VEC), a major animal hospital in Toronto, and had an appointment with her the following Tuesday. Like Eglinton Veterinary Facility, VEC is a superb place with great people.

The next day, Friday before a long weekend, I had to go out of town — a one hour drive for my work — to meet with a client, a wonderful man who has adopted many animals and who shared an amazing rescue story with me. On my drive back, around 1 p.m. on a very busy expressway, the phone rings. It is Helen screaming. She and Benjamin are in a park close to home, Benjamin having pulled her two blocks at full speed, looking for grass to eat and then vomiting several times. She had to get him to the vet immediately. I speed-dialled a taxi driver I know but he was in another part of the city. Concurrently, Helen called our building and Pirahal, our concierge supervisor, immediately drove over to the park to pick her and Benjamin up and took them home, at which point Helen got the car and sped Benjamin to our vet.

I drove through the city and got there about 15 minutes later, just in time to observe the examination — and to receive the most shocking news imaginable. Benjamin's lymph nodes were swollen and Dr. Hodges suspected he had cancer. She took a fine needle aspirate sample.

We were distressed beyond words, in a state of anguish and disbelief. We immediately booked an appointment with the oncologist at VEC; however, with the long weekend, the earliest we could get was the next Wednesday, a five day wait for the aspirate test results. For the same reason, we couldn't get stool sample results either. Waiting thorough the long weekend seemed like an eternity. We tried calling the two labs — stool test and cell sample — both were closed for the weekend.

Tuesday night the phone rings. It's the neurologist, Dr. Cochrane, on the line. She was at the clinic and had just received Benjamin's fine needle aspirate test results. Dr. Hodges' suspicion was correct

— Benjamin had lymphoma. I was distraught on the phone, and we both went to pieces after the call. The anguish was too much to bear. But being the supersensitive creature that he is, this alarmed Benjamin and I knew that I, in particular, needed to get myself together.

Wednesday morning we're back at VEC seeing Dr. Doug Mason, the internist. Dr. Kevin Finora, Oncologist, is off but Doug and our own vets wanted Benjamin to be seen and a treatment plan started immediately. Doug had seen Benjamin a year earlier for an elevated liver enzyme count which appeared in a routine annual check-up, and had prescribed a daily liver pill, which Benjamin has been on since.

Doug, with an intern in tow, examined Benjamin and pronounced that he was a perfect candidate for chemotherapy but it had to begin immediately. Doug very patiently answered our many questions, dealt with great sensitivity with our emotional state, and we got the treatment under way.

We had about forty five minutes waiting time, so Helen and I walked to a coffee shop a couple of blocks away for some ice tea and oatmeal cookies on a blisteringly hot day, to talk about our new reality.

If your pet begins to exhibit any signs which are out of the ordinary, call or see your vet. There could be any number of reasons, hopefully nothing to worry about at all. Moreover, the results of a physical exam, and stool and/or blood test may be fine. It could be as simple as your pet eating something off the ground or otherwise picking up an easily treatable parasite.

That said, and not to scare you unduly, recurring symptoms could be an indication of an underlying physiological change. So, monitor any change in your pet's behaviour or physiology carefully.

In the interim, at least you will have the benefit of a physical exam and possibly testing to hopefully determine a clear course of action for your pet's malady, or otherwise give you some peace of mind.

Rollercoaster

Saturday, July 14, 2012, 4:10 p.m. Another brutally hot day.

Benjamin's lying on the cool marble floor of the lobby of our condo building, head resting on his outstretched right paw, sleeping soundly just across from the concierge desk, having had a nice rub down by Andy who is one of the officers on duty. I am sitting on a comfortable chair, catching up on some sleep having been out with Benjamin at 3 a.m. for a bout of post-chemo diarrhea.

We are learning from our internet research, and visits with and countless calls to our vets at Eglinton Vet and VEC, that we are engaged in a process — the 25-week Madison Wisconsin Protocol of nine weekly treatments followed by 16 bi-weekly treatments, that there are side effects, that it will make our little boy tired, and that this is our new reality until he has recovered.

The great news is, after one treatment, Benjamin is in remission!

Anyone who has dealt with illness, in this case, as a caregiver to a loved one, knows the emotional ups and downs on a daily basis as the patient's condition changes. In Benjamin's situation, the side effects of chemo, combined with the brutally hot weather — which was never his favourite — have us in a constant state of alert. In particular, one of the side effects of chemo which Benjamin is experiencing is diarrhea, which causes us to worry to no end even though our vet says not to.

Aside from the impact on our little boy — it must be exhausting for him — we are also running out in the middle of the night, and continually trying to calibrate meals, cutting back on some ingredients, adding rice, administering medication.

Yesterday, Helen made boiled chicken and Benjamin loved it! But I also administered anti-diarrhea pills, which I had to cut to get the three-quarter tablet prescribed dosage. The scent and taste of the exposed compound is extremely bitter and Benjamin spit it out on the floor. I forced him to eat it wrapped in some meat and rice, causing him terrible distress — you get the picture. I vowed never to do that again.

A call to the clinic, a consult with the doctor on duty, an order of liquid anti-diarrhea medication for administration using a syringe — very stressful also — and a further order of medication in the precise tablet size.

It has been two years since I developed the idea for The Benjamin Project and have done any writing for this book. I wrote the first six chapters in the spring/summer of 2010, and then my usual deplorable workaholic tendencies took over and I haven't had the time or energy to do anything more.

A wise person once said, "A crisis is a terrible thing to waste." For the first time in ages — one of the first times ever for me — I am engaged in a truly meaningful and sustained way in the care of a loved one. For one of the first times, I am determined to stick with something of true importance to me besides work.

As I write this, I am sitting in the lobby of our condo at 2:17 p.m. Sunday, July 15, 2012. Benjamin is resting peacefully on the cool marble floor, passing residents giving him a gentle rub. They are enthralled and he is so happy.

Reading the Signs

It's 10 p.m. July 19, 2012. Benjamin has been lethargic all day but also agitated. Continually wanting to lie in the hallway just outside our door, which we now have open most of the time (again, at the indulgence of wonderful neighbours who love Benjamin and have no objection).

I am increasingly concerned to the point I take Benjamin down to the VEC. He is "triaged" immediately by a technician but we are only seen by the emergency room vet on duty at 2:30 a.m. Waiting seemed an eternity. I am anxious — unsure about his condition, wondering if I am doing the right thing by even being there. The vet examines Benjamin and runs blood tests. Everything tests out fine! He is A-okay!

Sunday, July 22, 10 a.m. I go to pick up Benjamin's night jersey from his bed for the wash. The jersey is completely wet. My anxiety goes through the roof, as I have never seen this before. I call the VEC but, of course, this being the weekend, our specialists are not on duty. Helen and I discuss the matter — tears running down my face — I think this may be a sign of incontinence related to the medications.

A reassuring call with Dr. Bateman at Eglinton Vet the next morning sets my mind at ease. In all likelihood, Benjamin's position when sleeping was one such that he experienced some seepage but it was very doubtful that he had incontinence.

The symptoms of lethargy and agitation, as well as panting, heavy peeing, occasional diarrhea, some seepage, being very thirsty, continue. We begin to understand from discussions with Drs. Bob, Kevin, and their colleagues, that these are side effects of the chemo and the Prednisone. We still worry, but at least we are better able to read the signs.

Being Present

Our greatly anticipated summer vacation at a country house on a quiet side road on a beautiful, quiet spring fed lake in the Laurentians, where the three of us love to unwind, walk, hike in forests abundant with deer, pick wild raspberries, cook and eat well, read, watch movies — an idyllic life in a spectacular setting — is gone for this year. Much too long a trip for our little guy under the circumstances and impossible given his weekly treatments, and far too hot this summer.

But we have each other. We are all in this together. We are going to get through this and that is all that counts.

Finding the Patterns

July 22, 2012. Our newly-scheduled visit to the clinic for Benjamin's second chemo treatment, last week's having been postponed because of a low white blood count.

Helen, Benjamin and I arrive at 11:50 a.m. for our appointment. Benjamin has been fasting, which we subsequently learned was not a requirement for chemo. Nonetheless, he is in good spirits and pulls Helen into the clinic with his tail wagging! The waiting room was virtually empty and we're seen promptly at noon.

After a brief discussion with Dr. Kevin, updating on Benjamin's status — answering Kevin's questions and having our questions answered as well: "There are 30 I.U. in the Alaska salmon fish oil capsules we bought for Benjamin — is this okay?" (Answer: "Yes"); "If we are not supposed to take Benjamin to dog parks because of the risk of infection, does that mean I shouldn't take him to the pet store either?" (Answer: "No pet store for the duration of treatment.")

Kevin does a physical exam and reports that Benjamin's lymph nodes are fine! We are worried that Benjamin has lost weight, but Kevin assures us that his weight is fine and all other signs are perfect. Benjamin is led off by Dr. Francesca DiMauro, Kevin's intern, for his blood tests and chemo. We wait in the waiting area.

I spend the time praying for an elevated white blood count so that Benjamin can have his treatment. I also meditate and send light to surround my little boy as five minutes becomes 10, then 20, and then Michael, the technician, and Benjamin come bounding through the door into the waiting area at full clip! Michael has a cookie for Benjamin which I didn't want him to get — we cut out commercial treats several years earlier because of Benjamin's tummy troubles — but he is *famished* so I relent. Michael tells us that Benj's blood count is normal — on the high side of normal, in fact, which is great! His weight is actually up a tad from last week. We are elated. Benjamin is starved when we get home and eats ravenously. However, this particular dose of chemo really knocks him out and he sleeps much of the next 24 hours. We have two outings just to pee, the sun and heat being detriments to staying outdoors. Nevertheless, Benjamin's appetite is good, and, as Dr. Bob continues to remind us, "A good appetite is a great sign!"

The Prednisone kicks in around 4 p.m., the usual three to four hours later, and Benj is agitated through the evening until midnight — continually wanting to go out. Each time, I put on my sandals and grab his leash, water and waist pouch with poo bags and cell phone, but most of the time Benjamin just wants to lie in the hallway outside our door. We are blessed with great neighbours; Evelyn right next door cheerfully makes her way around Benjamin, and if he sees Lynne across the hall or Aliza, Francoise, Garian or Maureen from the units way down the hall, Benjamin's in one of their suites in a flash! Benjamin literally jumps off his feet and tears over to Lynne whenever he sees her, and scampers back to our unit on his own from the far end of the floor after visiting with Aliza for a small piece of rye bread, tags jingling all the way.

I'm a very light sleeper and have been since the day we got Benjamin. My extreme work habits over the years have further conditioned me to getting by on very little sleep, not a good thing by any means. At 3:30 a.m. I'm listening and straining my eyes in the dark to see if I can spot Benjamin on his bed. Not seeing him nor hearing him, I get up to check; he immediately bounces up from sleeping on the carpet right next to the bed and wants to go out! A long pee (side effect from the Prednisone) and a big soft poo and back upstairs.

Many times in the past, Benj would lick his chops on the ride up in the elevator after a poo, even in the middle of the night, telling me in no uncertain terms "I'm hungry!", but this time he heads right to one of his beds (the one in the family room), and goes to sleep. I do the same.

The next morning after a short walk around 7 a.m. — yes, I slept in! — I head down to the small fitness room in my building. I have been too tired — and the weather has been too hot — to run outside for several weeks, which is really bad for me. Running is a big stress release and keeps me in some semblance of shape. The elliptical and rowing machines, plus free weights are good compensation, though, and I have a decent workout. After breakfast, it's a full day of chores and looking after Benjamin.

It's a little cooler and Benjamin wants to be out a lot, go on short walks, or just lie outside the front door of our building, in the lobby, and of course in the hallway outside our unit. All day and through the evening, I find Benj less agitated this time, possibly still fatigued from this round of chemo — but it requires constant vigilance and caregiving on our part until I finally turn in around 11 p.m. Helen stays up to take Benjamin out one more time.

Saturday, July 29. Benjamin sleeps in and so do I — to 6 a.m. this time. Today is a glorious day, the sun is coming up and it's cool — this is our kind of weather! After a long pee, Benjamin and I head down the street on a brisk walk. Benjamin pulls me to the parkette and is sniffing like mad at one spot, until it dawns on me that it could be a scent from raccoons. I pull him away out of concern for infection. We head north on Yonge Street past Pet Valu, across and then south past Shoppers Drugs and Tim Horton's — I'm following Benjamin on one of his many self-selected routes and he is on a tear! What a wonderful feeling.

Side Effects

Friday, August 17, 2012. We head down to the clinic for Benjamin's weekly treatment. Benjamin's white blood count has come way up, which is great news! And he has put on a bit of weight! We are through within 20 minutes and head home, stopping briefly for Helen to pick up her favourite ground coffee blend at a nearby supermarket. We are feeling great about things.

But this time, the side effects from the chemo hit with a vengeance. In addition to enormous fatigue, compounded by the unbearable heat and a thick and increasingly shaggy coat — no grooming until a particular two-day window in the treatment cycle — Benjamin has had diarrhea for several days; and worse still, won't eat. This strikes terror in us and we are worried sick. Moreover, the diarrhea and nausea pills that were prescribed previously have to be cut to get the right dosage for him — one-half of the Metronidazole for diarrhea; three-quarters of the Metoclopramaide pill for nausea.

Benjamin smells the compounds immediately and won't take the medications. Wrapping them in his favourite cheese doesn't work, nor does peanut butter. We are beside ourselves. We call the clinic and speak with Francesca, one of Kevin's interns, and arrange for a refill of the liquid form for both medications for administration orally using a syringe. I head down to the clinic to get the meds.

By now I have modified my technique, and proceed to give Benj the respective medications very gently and nonchalantly, so that he isn't spooked and has time to swallow the .5 millilitre of Metronidazole and 1.7 millilitre of Metoclopramaide gently — as compared to administering the full amount quickly as we had been.

By Tuesday, I am frantic as Benjamin's condition isn't improving and he still isn't eating. I call Kevin, who assures me that these side effects are normal and that Benjamin's appetite will return. Concurrently, I drop by the pet store and learn of a "pill pocket" treat expressly to alleviate the trauma of administering oral medication and pick up several bags.

Helen and I do another round of cooking — boiled chicken, baked salmon, steamed potatoes, and Benjamin's old favourites: hard boiled and scrambled eggs. One of these has to work! And steadily and surely Benjamin's appetite returns! And the side effects stop.

We are incredibly relieved and happy. I am able to fit in some more concentrated work during the day, and get a couple of nights sleep for five hours straight. Bliss!

If you or someone you know has experienced cancer, you will recognize the side effects from medications readily, for they are virtually the same for 'four-legged' people as for two-legged. Fatigue, nausea, diarrhea are common, and incredible agitation from Prednisone in particular.

Within a short time after taking his Prednisone, Benjamin will begin to hyperventilate and want to lie in the hallway and come back countless times to get me to stay out there with him! This can go on for many hours, until exhaustion sets in (for both of us!). Be prepared for the side effects. Keep a log to record when to administer the meds. Don't leave the timing to memory — you will have too much else going on. Greenie "pill pockets" are a godsend!

Discuss any concerns in a timely manner with your oncologist — in our case, we also keep our regular vet informed, who is always interested in Benjamin's welfare.

Be prepared for a significant impact on your time and/or 'lifestyle' — taking care of an infirm loved one (two- or four-legged) is a full time job! You will need help, or something will have to go.

Rollercoaster 2

Friday, August 24. The day of our weekly visit to the clinic. This is a break week though — the first five treatments have been completed, so Benjamin has a "bye" for a two-week period. Today's visit is for the usual examination and blood test.

We are very hopeful about things, given that Benjamin recovered from the side effects from last week's chemo. But our anxiety skyrockets when his blood test results show a very low white cell count. His weight is also down to 16 kilograms or 35.2 pounds, lower than the week before and several pounds below what his weight was when this all started.

Not being medically trained, these results strike fear and anguish within us. However Kevin, Benjamin's oncologist, is his usual unflappable self and makes it clear he isn't worried. He prescribes another round of antibiotics for the next week — the second round in five weeks — and we head home to feed Benjamin and initiate this medication.

Thankfully, Benjamin's appetite is very strong and he relishes his meals (pardon the pun!) with all the home cooking. We are determined to keep nurturing him, body and soul, to give him a chance to recover, boost his white blood count, and be ready for his next treatment.

Breakthrough

Sunday, September 2, 2012, Labour Day weekend. The weather is spectacular: cool mornings and dry sunny days. Benjamin is on a tear on his morning walk, pulling me off my feet. His appetite is excellent, gorging on a combination of free range organic barbecue chicken — a new favourite; homemade chicken burgers with shredded carrots, parsley and zucchini; and caught-in-the-wild pacific salmon (plus toast and cheese for his late night snack; morsels of rye bread and rice cakes from Aliza down the hall and Lynne across the way; and tidbits of thick homemade peanut butter and molasses health bars with tons of nuts and cranberries — yes, and a little brown sugar for good measure.)

So far, Benjamin has had very few side effects since his Friday treatment — just tiredness during the day — and he musters up the energy to pull me a good few blocks to the Baptist church, a beautiful edifice on a very large property with benches and picnic tables. This being the last long weekend of summer, the city is very quiet with so many people away. Benjamin lies down on the grass watching the world go by — something he can do for *hours* — and I sit at a table reading the paper. What a treat! This is the most relaxation I have had in months.

Benjamin's appetite is great. His energy is up. His spirits are lifted. And so are ours. I feel we have turned a corner, and we are on a path to complete recovery.

Friday January 11, 2013. Benjamin's last treatment! The past couple of weeks have seen the "usual" side effects including a rough patch the second week of this two-week interval, and Helen and I are apprehensive about another treatment under the circumstances. But, Benjamin is on the rebound and Kevin is firm about not delaying the last treatment.

Benjamin's blood test results are fine, his physiology is perfect, so the last treatment proceeds.

A phone conversation the next day with Kim, a receptionist at VEC, whose own dog had gone through chemotherapy, convinced me to hold off giving diarrhea medication preventatively as it could cause constipation; so over the next week or so I gave Benjamin meds only as symptoms manifested themselves.

Before I forget, I want to acknowledge the incredible staff at both Eglinton Veterinary and Veterinary Emergency Clinic. Cheryl, Kasey, Melanie, Sandra, Sharon, Blair, and Dalton at Eglinton, and Allison, Dave, Kate, Kim, Laura, Katerina, Michael, Mindey, Morgan, Natasha, Sandra and Sansha at VEC are all terrific people and have been exceptionally helpful to us throughout this ordeal, and, in the case of Eglinton, for many years.

As I write this on February 2, 2013, Benjamin is doing great. Aside from a few days of rain ("the January thaws", as my late dad used to say), the cold weather agrees with Benj to a "T". His energy is high, walks are very long and Benjamin's appetite is off the charts. This morning we were out at 4:15 for an urgent somewhat soft poo, another one at 7:30, and several more walks on this blistering cold day. But we are happy!

I suspect today's tummy trouble may be a function of my feeding Benjamin a bit too many morsels of toast and cheese, noodles, crackers, baked salmon, and whatever else we may have eaten through the course of the day yesterday. I am hopelessly unable to resist his big bright eyes and wagging tail as he rests his chin on my knee at the kitchen table asking for food.

It's now 8:15 p.m. Benjamin is sleeping soundly after his *fifth* meal today, the last one featuring Helen's boiled chicken and chicken soup. And, what with the walks, the bitter cold, carrying Benj at times due to the blasted salt, and meal preparations, I'm also exhausted! But we are ecstatic. Our little boy is fine. His final report from Dr. Kevin, which I got from Dr. Bob Thursday evening, is unequivocal:

"Benjamin is in complete remission and he is doing well." We are all moving forward together — me, Helen and Benjamin. Benj resumes his favourite pastime — playing with other doggies. He has made it through with flying colours. Life is good.

The rest of the winter and early spring went spectacularly well.

Helen's Homemade Chicken Burgers
Makes 6 Big Patties!

½ lb. white and ½ lb. dark ground chicken
1 egg
¼ cup bread crumbs
1 large carrot, shredded
1 large zucchini, shredded

Mix all ingredients in a large bowl, gradually adding the bread crumbs.

Place 6 round patties on a cookie sheet covered with parchment paper.

Bake at 400° F for 10 minutes. Flip and bake for 10 more minutes and voilá!

Caution!

There are differing opinions as to the merits of antioxidants and nutritional supplements for pets with cancer, so I suggest you discuss these with your vet prior to administering them.

Veterinary Emergency Clinic and Referral Centre
920 Yonge Street, Suite #117, Toronto Ontario M4W 3C7
Phone #: (416) 920-2002   Fax #: (416) 920-6185

Kevin Finora, DVM, Diplomate ACVIM (Oncology and Small Animal Internal Medicine)
Consultations in Oncology and Internal Medicine

Case Summary Oncology Referral:

Jan 11, 2013

Referring Veterinarian: Robert John Watson, DVM , Eglinton Veterinary Facilities. Fax: 416-642-1012
Attending Oncologist: Kevin Finora DVM, Diplomate ACVIM (Oncology and Small Animal Internal Medicine).

Patient: "Benjamin" Brent.   **Case Number:** 11-2109

Dear Dr. Watson;

Thank you for the referral of Benjamin Brent. He is a neutered male, Terrier Mix, and is 12 years & 8 months old.

History: On July 3, 2012 Benjamin was seen by the neurology and internal medicine service. No neurological abnormalities were identified. Peripheral lymphadenopathy was identified and abdominal ultrasound was performed and revealed 2-3 enlarged mesenteric lymph nodes. Cytology confirmed a diagnosis of lymphoma, minimum Stage IIIa He is currently being treated with Madison-Wisconsin protocol. He was noted to have a decreased appetite for most of the last two weeks. His energy level has remained good.

Physical Examination: Upon physical exam Benjamin no abnormalities were detected on thoracic auscultation. The lymph nodes were normal. No other abnormalities were noted on physical exam.

Diagnosis: Lymphoma, multicentric (minimum Stage III)

Diagnostics and Results: CBC: Safe and appropriate for the administration of chemotherapy.

Treatment: Today Benjamin was treated with doxorubicin.

Medication: Metronidazole (250mg) ¾ tablet can be given orally q12hours if diarrhea develops
Metoclopramide (10mg) ½ tablet can be given orally q12hours if vomiting occurs subsequent to treatment

Recommendations: Benjamin is doing well. I am pleased with how he is doing. He is in complete remission. He did well for his treatment today. Benjamin has now finished his chemotherapy protocol. I have instructed the owners to evaluate the submandibular lymph nodes on a weekly basis. I will now recheck Benjamin on a monthly basis. He will be due back for his next visit in four weeks.

Thank you for the referral of this case. If you have any questions or concerns, please do not hesitate to contact me.

Sincerely,

Kevin Finora DVM, Diplomate ACVIM (Oncology and Small Animal Internal Medicine)

Dogs in Cars

It's mid-spring 2013 and the warmer weather is beginning.

We hear increasingly, and alarmingly so, of people leaving infants in cars with catastrophic outcomes and we are horrified. How can this happen? I don't pass judgment, though. The unspeakable tragedy notwithstanding, I can see how, with the craziness of our lives — the overwhelming stress and distraction — a parent can strap a toddler into his or her car seat in the back of the car, get to their destination at which point the infant is fast asleep, and leave to grab the train, subway, or go into their place of work.

I have no such empathy for people who leave their pet locked in their car, especially with even the slightest semblance of warm weather. There is no excuse for this, and leaving the windows open one or two inches doesn't make it right!

On several occasions, Helen and/or I have left bluntly worded notes on windshields even when it seemed a pet locked in a car was okay, because the practice is just plain wrong. On two occasions we called the police. Once on holiday in St. Jovite, Quebec, in the vicinity of our summer vacation spot, we saw two small dogs in a car parked in the midday sun with no windows open! Very shortly after we placed a call to the local police, an officer drove up, checked the owner's coordinates through a central database, walked in to the pharmacy which, fortunately, the parking lot belonged to, and came out with an older man in tow. Somewhat immaturely, in hindsight, I was still standing there and had a sharp exchange with this gentleman. In any case, I'm sure he won't leave his dogs like that again.

The second time occurred some four or five summers ago. Again, a very hot sunny day, two dogs parked in a car with no windows open, whom Helen spotted by chance on a walk a block away from our building. She called me and I ran over; we called the police who came quickly, traced the car to a registration in another city, and, with no owner in sight, smashed the driver side window, opened the door, and let these two seriously dehydrated dogs out. We got bowls of water from the nearest house, the dogs were taken to the municipal animal services, and the car impounded. About an hour later, just as the police had finished their onsite report and a local TV crew had interviewed Helen (which she agreed to reluctantly), the owner came up, shopping bags in hand, and professed that she had only been gone 15 minutes! We let the police handle this one.

(I followed up several times with the municipal animal service and was assured that the owner had been in touch and would be retrieving their dogs the next day).

I give great credit and thanks to the two officers involved in this last instance, the officer in St. Jovite, and police and firemen everywhere who take this so seriously. And to TV channels who put on public service announcements about this, although I wish *all* TV and radio stations, and other media, would include a "dogs and little people" weather advisory *daily* from at least April to October.

If you see a pet locked in a closed car on a warm let alone hot day, even one with windows open, do something about it. Call the police, minimally leave a sharply worded note. It becomes your responsibility at that point, since someone else didn't take theirs as they should.

See the Ontario SPCA's website _hotpets.ca_ for your pledge to not leave your pet in a vehicle.

We have a duty of kindness to all animals.

We have a duty to prevent cruelty to all animals.

We have a duty of humane treatment towards all animals, which includes that euthanasia should be considered only as a last resort after all other options have been exhausted and then only in the case of irremediable pain or loss of a significant quality of life, or if the animal is a proven and significant danger to the safety of the public.

We hold that animals who become human companions should be treated with respect, dignity and valued for their social interaction and contribution to humanity, such that they should not be considered simple property, but rather sentient, living creatures in their own right.

We hold that human caretakers of animals and potential caretakers are to be highly valued and considered as partners in our ongoing efforts to educate the general public on the inherent value of animals, including the need to spay or neuter in order to reduce suffering in the urban wilds.

We hold that we as humans have a responsibility for the animals whom we have domesticated, and that we will strive for an Animal Bill of Rights that reflects all of the above.

From the Toronto Humane Society at the time of its founding by John J. Kelso February 24, 1887

Reflections

All told, the fall has been good, with the usual ups and downs, but generally Benjamin is doing great. With the onset of the cooler weather in November, his energy has been way up and we have been going on some very long walks — as long as we used to — at a very good clip!

Treatments have been relatively smooth, with more pronounced side effects from certain chemo drugs, but we now know what to expect and that helps. The great news is that Benjamin's appetite is incredibly good and his blood tests are excellent. He's had two groomings since Labour Day. Given his condition, we had to curtail the grooming with Jennifer to whom he had been going to for years at John Andrew for Pets, because of all the other dogs there and hence the risk of Benjamin getting an infection.

So we started having him groomed by Justin at Pet Valu, Benjamin's favourite store just down the street. Justin disinfects his Groomingdale's boutique in the store the night before, and he takes Benjamin first thing in the morning when no other dogs are present. Justin is very caring and gives Benjamin a great cut, and Benjamin is now looking as good as ever — soft fur, nicely trimmed, beautiful rust-coloured hue with grey and black flecks. And, best of all, Benj is back to going into the pet store — admittedly under controlled conditions, until a month after his last treatment January 11, 2013. Then, he will be ready to resume all his normal activities!

Saturday, December 1, 2012. A dreary, grey Toronto day. Benjamin had two long walks nonetheless, and one short outing up and down Yonge Street in our neighbourhood, got lots of compliments as usual

— "He's so cute!"; "With soft fur!"; "What a beautiful face!", and he has eaten his homemade chicken burgers ravenously. Benjamin is very tired tonight, though — the side effects of yesterday's chemo treatment — which was the start of his final biweekly four-treatment cycle.

Helen's health has been poor this fall, some days good and many not. But she continues to persevere, takes great care of Benjamin, cooks for him almost daily, and walks her feet off given his generally very high energy.

January 8, 2013. The past week has been rough for Benjamin. The side effects from his last treatment have been pronounced, we've been out in the middle of the night two nights in a row and many times during the day, with much of the days spent sitting with him in the hallway at his *express* request to comfort him — all the while trying to get some work done (there are many times when Benjamin wants to lie in the hallway because of agitation, which we suspect is a reaction to the chemo, and definitely because it's a lot cooler due to the air circulation system — and he will run back into our unit to get me at my desk, put his head on my knee with tail wagging and facial expression very animated, telling me he wants me out in the hallway with him right now! So I gather up whatever I'm working on and go. Don't even ask about my 'productivity'. (Thank goodness for the occasional sitting relief provided by Jennifer, Kasey, and Sharon, dog lovers all who help us out every so often.) A sore and at times excruciating left knee, which I now have, injured on what was a rare outside run these days, isn't helping matters.

But, even with all this, Benjamin has taken us on some long walks over the past week and, with the benefit of his meds, can be enticed for his meals quite nicely with Helen's chicken soup with big pieces of chicken and carrots, which he polishes off in no time. It's really wonderful to see.

January 11, 2013. Benjamin's last treatment! While Helen and I are apprehensive about another treatment so soon after his last bout of side effects, Benjamin is on the rebound and Kevin is firm about not postponing the last treatment. We're greeted at VEC by Doctor Robin McCrae, another of Kevin's ever cheerful interns, and

Kevin does his usual examination prior to a blood test. Benjamin's blood tests results are fine, his physiology is perfect, so the treatment proceeds.

A helpful phone conversation on January 12 with Kim, an attendant at VEC whose own dog had gone through chemo, convinced me to hold off giving Benjamin diarrhea medication as a preventative measure as it could cause constipation.

As I write this on February 3, 2013, Benjamin is doing great. Aside from a few days of rain ("the January thaws" as my late dad used to say), the cold weather agrees with Benj to a "T". His energy is high, walks are *very* long! and Benjamin's appetite is off the charts. Yesterday morning mind you, we were out at 4:15 for an urgent somewhat soft poo, and another increasingly soft one at 7:30 this evening after a number of outings on a blustery cold day; followed by the onset of a diarrhea-type situation on another urgent outing at 12:15 this morning. This time, however, I wonder whether Benjamin's tummy troubles may be a function of my feeding him a bit too many morsels of toast and cheese, noodles, crackers, baked salmon, and whatever else we may have been eating over the last day or so due to his insistence on partaking and my inability to say no.

We were out again at 5:15 this morning for another urgent situation, but even at that, I marvel at how Benjamin can run and get me, wait for me to bundle up, and exert so much self-control until we get outside. As I sit here writing this, about an hour later, he is lying on one his beds right next to my chair in my office, sound asleep. I am enthralled just watching him. Benjamin's final report from Kevin, which we got when we went in to see Bob at Eglinton Veterinary yesterday, is an equivocal bill of good health: *"Benjamin is in complete remission and is doing well."* We will see Kevin monthly for a check up for the next eight months.

We're all moving forward together — me, Helen and Benjamin. Within a week or so, Benj can resume his favourite pastime — playing with other dogs! He has made it through with flying colours. Life is good.

We heard on the news recently about an Ontario Court of Appeal judge who overturned the City of Toronto law banning the use of shark fins in restaurants (due to the extreme cruelty involved in slaughtering these creatures) because four restaurant owners want to keep using fins in their soup recipes. Helen fires off an e-mail to our local municipal counsellor, expressing our dismay and asking what City Council will do about this. And, we despair at the lack of enlightenment of the people involved.

It's easy to get despondent if you let things get to you: Political polarization; environmental degradation — the news yesterday profiled an even greater and far more ominous degree of ice cap melting than was previously thought to be the case; war zones with unspeakable horrors … there's plenty of bad news to go around. But there's also the good side of things. The economy slowly and very grudgingly inching back; the recent U.S. "fiscal cliff" crisis averted; uplifting YouTube videos just posted about a pet deer and its love affair with a family's cat; another photo posted recently of a 19-year old arthritic German Shepherd asleep in his owner's arms in the warm water on a beautiful summer's day.

We saw a segment on ABC News the evening of January 23. It's a video shot by scuba divers in a tropical ocean who came upon a dolphin in distress, swam over to find him entangled in free floating netting, and took eight precious minutes to painstakingly cut off the horrible encumbrance. The rescued dolphin swam off, circled back to literally cuddle with the divers, and then swam off for good. A beautiful, sensitive, and incredibly intelligent and intuitive creature. Another rescued Benjamin.

We in our family are not immune from the stress and strains of everyday life. Like many people, we rail against things that offend our sensibilities, work too hard, complain about the small stuff, get fatigued at times, are unable to get to some personal matters or even mundane ones — such as dropping off some old clothes to a charity or an old bed of Benjamin's to a shelter, all of which have been in the back seat of the car for months! But in our more 'lucid' moments, we try not to let these mundane trials and tribulations get in the way of the things that really count.

In our case, that revolves around our very special little boy, Benjamin. Regardless of how stressed, tired or preoccupied you are, he is always right there by your side — literally. When he curls up in one of his beds at night, and we wrap him up in a toasty fleece right out of the dryer and see the sheer bliss on his face, we are enthralled.

When he takes us on a long excursion, tail wagging, sniffing everywhere and, as was the case recently, barking and chasing his tail for the first time in many months, we are overjoyed. When he comes asking for his mid-afternoon carrot, and crunches away with his big teeth and big bright eyes looking up at us, we never cease to be amazed.

When he lets strangers pat him — as everyone young and old who sees him wants to do — we know how lucky we are to have such a wonderful little pup in our lives.

This book is in honour of Benjamin, but it is also a testament to all the Benjamins in the world — four-legged, two-winged, dorsal-finned, sentient beings all, many living in horrible conditions, others fortunate to live in loving circumstances — or, if not, hopefully just waiting for someone to give them a wonderful home, so that they can shower their new family with unconditional love.

I hope you have enjoyed this short story and that you feel good knowing that all proceeds from its sale, after the cost of printing and distribution, are going to an animal welfare organization, to do justice to all these wonderful creatures and to, in some small way, do what they do so well — make the world a better place.

"*They are angels in our midst, pure goodness, without guile, without vengeance or malice or pride, attentive and capable of selfless love in ways that we (as humans) can only apire to.*"

Alex Colville, Canadian painter, speaking in Toronto in 1994.

The Difficult Part

Sunday, June 9, 2013, 3 a.m. Benjamin and I had just got back from a leisurely walk on rather a nice night, after several weeks of unsettled and unseasonably cool weather in this climatically challenged spring across North America and Europe. He pawed my bedside about 45 minutes ago, which I tweaked to after a slight delay, being ever the light sleeper but in somewhat of a stupor at the time. Fortunately, for once, I went to bed at 10:30 last night as compared to my continued customary midnight, 1 or 2 a.m. So I wasn't too tired nor cranky waking up.

You see, two months ago, Benjamin's lymphoma returned, so he has been on chemo and Prednisone since with all the side effects I have already described. The symptoms were the same — snoring, diahrrea, panting; and again, blood tests were normal. However, one day, just by fluke, I felt a pronounced lump in Benjamin's neck when playing with him as the three of us walked down the corridor to the elevator for our nightly outing; and our fears and anxieties returned instantly. The wait — again, on a long weekend like the first time — was distressing; and the past eight weeks exhausting — many middle-of the-night outings, many visits to the clinic for treatments (the clinic/hospital still operating out of its North Toronto branch — a long drive with a sick doggie — until the South branch, quite close to our home, reopens in a couple of weeks after last winter's water main burst, which almost destroyed the entire building and necessitated the emergency evacuation of over 100 pets in the middle of a bitterly cold night).

Fortunately, Benjamin is responding very well to treatments since they resumed May 14, side effects aside. And, the cooler intemperate spring has to this point been a godsend — as compared to the brutally hot spring and summer we had last year.

The week, though, has been difficult. Benjamin had another collapse while at the clinic on Wednesday for his bi-weekly treatment. The good news, though, aside from a quick recovery from the incident, was that Kevin, Benjamin's oncologist, had an ECG done immediately and it showed a slight irregular heartbeat which seemed a plausible cause of this type of intermittent incident. We also booked Benjamin with a cardiologist, Dr. Regan Williams, for a heart ultrasound and 24-hour Holter monitor, as Kevin wanted the results prior to the next treatment. This necessitated us going back to the clinic the next day, which we were loathe to do given Benjamin's fatigue and the heat wave we were having at the time; however, Kevin wanted the results from both the ultrasound and heart monitor prior to the next weekly chemo treatment, so we complied. Regan was assisted by Kristin and Roseanne, and we observed the ultrasound in real time on Thursday — thank God Benjamin's heart is fine; and he had the heart monitor put on — not a straightforward procedure! Shaving his chest a bit, wrapping the monitor in place with lots of tape in a very intricate manner.

We then had to trek back up to the clinic the next evening, taxing Benjamin's energy even more, to have the monitor removed. This is not a simple thing to do — there were lots of connectors glued to Benjamin's chest, very intricate bandaging, some of it sticking to Benjamin's fur. Oscar, the technician was excellent — confident, kind, compassionate. But it still took a solid half-hour and Benjamin was increasingly fatigued. We were very happy when the monitor and all attachments and electrodes were off, and we could head home.

Benjamin and I went out at eight this morning, as a beautiful day was starting to unfold. Now, as I sit at noon in the warm brilliant sunshine on the church steps on our quiet street, across from our building, with Benjamin a few feet away in the shade watching the world go by, I can revel in this moment of tranquility and reflection. Our overarching anxiety about Benj over the past eight weeks;

the stress of turning out deliverables at work on no sleep; a kitchen reno after 12 years of talking about it, which started around the same time as Benjamin's diagnosis — the last thing we needed under the circumstances, but the work thankfully has gone well and is almost over; an excruciating knee — this time, courtesy of putting in one too many outdoor runs in a row, in a desperate attempt to keep my sanity — all of these melt away in the resplendent scene of sunshine and trees in full foliage, blue sky, birds chirping, and of course, people stopping to admire my beautiful little boy.

Saturday has been quiet, but I know I am facing a full day of work again on Sunday with no hope of getting through all of it. Still, I had nice breakfast an hour ago with Helen, also having had an hour off last night to go to a local restaurant, while a wonderful neighbour, Barbara, who loves Benjamin, sat with him — our first evening out in at least two months.

Saturday, June 29. 3:05 p.m. Much has happened over the past two weeks. Benjamin's cancer went into remission, but then recurred. His blood test results were good, however, so Kevin continued with the treatment. Two weeks ago, Benjamin had a seemingly particularly heavy duty chemo treatment which has caused a lot of fatigue and diahrrea. Moreover, we have had a blistering heat wave, which is the worst possible weather for Benjamin and hasn't made things easier. There have been many middle-of-the-night outings, and my fatigue continues to accumulate. Helen's too. Throughout, however, Benjamin's appetite has stayed great, as he devoured a variety of Helen's homemade cooking.

June 25 was a day we had identified with Kevin as okay for grooming, the prior week being a breakpoint in the treatment pro-tocol. I took Benjamin to the groomer's at the corner, but he was weak and wanted to run out of the pet store as we headed to the back where the grooming section is.

I stayed with him and had him washed only not cut, but it was a mistake I will never forgive myself for. He was whimpering, just as he did a year ago when I stayed for his wash elsewhere. He was very unhappy. *Why did I do this? Why did I force my little boy to go through this?* Based on the news we received the next day, I am distraught beyond words.

We went for his treatment the following day, and Benjamin's glands were swollen. We were seen initially by Kevin's intern Dr. Meghan Solc and Animal Care Assistant Kim prior to seeing Kevin. I am sure the distress of him being washed, quite vigorously at that, caused this (even though, when raising this with Kevin at a future appointment, he indicated that it was impossible — that I could not be a "cancer-causing agent".) Benjamin's white blood count was good so Kevin continued the treatment, but changed the protocol to an oral medication, which Benjamin will now receive every three weeks. Kevin also increased the Prednisone dosage, with the overwhelming heavy panting side effects.

Helen took Benjamin downstairs for some fresh air Thursday afternoon June 27 around 4 p.m., and he collapsed coming back into our building. Helen had not witnessed this first-hand before, and she was distraught — crying, pleading with Benjamin to respond while he lay prostrate in the middle of the floor in the foyer. Wonderful neighbours Elaine, Pauline and Josephine tried to help; and, as Benjamin started to respond, our concierge supervisor Pirahal picked him up — much as I have done when there have been other such occurrences, and rode up the elevator with Helen and Elaine, both of whom were crying. After a while, Benjamin regained his strength and, by then, I was racing home.

Benjamin is not doing well, so as soon as I get home at 5:30 we rush him to VEC where he is seen by Dr. Zoë Launcelott and two Animal Care assistants, Kim and Kendall, who take some preliminary vital signs prior to Dr. Erika Sullivan being available, and hold an oxygen hose in front of Benjamin's nose and mouth. We are sick with worry, but Benjamin has recovered enough for us to take him home to keep a close eye and do everything we can to help him recover.

June 30. The past three days have been increasingly bad. Benjamin has been very fatigued and he has virtually stopped eating. Thankfully, he still takes long drinks of water. Yesterday he lay in the hallway of our unit, not even near us. We have been increasingly worried and distraught beyond words. The pain of thinking of life without him is too great. I simply can't bear it.

I was out last night at around 11:30 p.m. and again in the middle of the night, and ended up sleeping until 7 a.m. Fortunately, it's Saturday of the Canada Day long weekend. I forced myself up, found Benjamin lying on one of his beds in my home office just next to our bedroom, and he was extremely weak. My anguish returns instantly. We are in and out four times by noon, diahrrea each time. But, with patience and persistence, Helen and I coax Benjamin to eat. Finger-fulls of peas and brown rice baby food, scrambled eggs, his canned food — all cold. He doesn't want anything warm. The last such "meal" about an hour ago, Benjamin ate from a very small bowl I held for him as he lay on his tummy on the marble floor. My heart soars with every mouthful.

In between, I get on the stationary bike — the same one we have had for 20 years — and did my own version of interval training, 10.8 miles in 30 minutes. I am cycling at this point because of its lower impact on my left knee, which still hurts, especially when lying down. But the exercise is great for it and for my wellbeing — I am drenched, energized, and vastly de-stressed.

It is now 8 p.m., Friday July 4, and I'm sitting in the carpeted hallway just outside the door of our unit. Benjamin is lying a little ways away, after having another mini-meal of some ground beef and noodles and some chicken noodle soup. My heart soared again when he ate. Helen and I have talked today, for the first time in ages, about things that matter — Benjamin's health, our lives, my work habits and the tolls those have taken. I am acutely aware that, at the end of the day, my work won't matter a damn. I really like it, and feel privileged to be able to do what I do; but nothing has nor ever will justify the time and effort I have put into it, regardless of how much I feel I have no choice or I will fail, and that the people I am doing this work for would be impacted accordingly.

I had an email exchange with Dr. Jaime Modiano, a vet oncologist at the University of Minnesota with whom I have corresponded occasionally in the past. I reached out to Jaime again today, desperate for some advice and hopefully positive feedback on this long weekend with none of our regular vets around. No, I do not begrudge that our wonderful vets are time off with their families. Moreover, Bob's colleague Dr. Bev Batemen has graciously provided us with their email address, which she mentioned she would check periodically, so I can't complain. They love Benjamin at Eglinton Vet, and everyone there is pulling for him.

Saturday July 5, 8 p.m. I'm sitting in the foyer of our building on this beautiful very warm night. Thankfully, it is very quiet — just Andy at the concierge desk and the occasional resident or guest. Benjamin just came in from an urgent episode of diahrrea, and is lying on the cool marble tiles. Fortunately, the chair I am in is very comfortable — a mini Louis XVIth, quite ergonomic!

Much of the past week has been very difficult — many urgent outings throughout the day and in the middle of the night; and three accidents in the hallway, fortunately all cleaned up without a trace. Work is busier than ever and I am getting further behind. Helen's stress and fatigue are both very high.

Benjamin's appetite was weak until Tuesday night when we had a breakthrough and he devoured three quarters of a can of his food in two 'helpings!' We were elated. The next day he ate again, although more so as the day progressed, and same Thursday. We are so happy, our hearts soar.

I have to drive out of town Thursday and I am planning to leave by 7:15 a.m. at the latest. However, an 'accident' in the hallway around 5:30 set me back; by the time I finished cleaning the carpet, disinfecting, and washing with vinegar to remove any odour, I left at 7:45, right in the middle of rush hour traffic on one of the busiest roadways in North America. My fatigue was such that I struggled to stay awake and actually missed the exit for Hamilton and ended up on the road to Niagara. Fortunately, there was one exit before the Skyway bridge otherwise I would have ended up countless kilometres away, so I took it, doubled back, and picked up the Hamilton-bound road.

Friday I had to be in Saskatoon, and opted to fly there and back the same day, not wanting to be away from Benjamin overnight. I slept like a log on the plane both ways, though much more so on the way out. In several conversations with Helen from the airport there, I learned that Benjamin wasn't eating again — he didn't want any food that morning either prior to my leaving for the airport at 6:30 a.m.

I am deeply worried. *'What am I doing here?'* I ask Helen. *'How can I be away for even a day under the circumstances? I never should have agreed to this — even with a prospective new customer. Benjamin is all that counts. When am I going to learn to say 'No!'*

Helen, exhausted as she was, was very supportive and told me there was no way I could hold myself responsible — that there was only so much I could control. But I was still anguished. And then shortly before boarding for the flight back, Helen called and told me that Benjamin had eaten a full meal! She had dashed out late that afternoon to get some lean ground veal — something we would typically never buy because of how the calves are raised — and cooked it for Benjamin in hopes of inducing him to eat. It did the trick — he polished it off. My mind is instantly at ease, my spirits are lifted. Everything is back on track.

Saturday morning, Benjamin let me sleep in until close to 8 a.m. It was around 12:30 a.m. by the time I got to bed, jet lagged. But today, Benjamin's energy is way up. For the first time in weeks, he took me on a walk down to the corner, up Yonge to the pet store (closed at this hour), across Yonge and down a bit, across again and home. His appetite was off the charts. Benjamin is alert, energetic, his tail wagging. We are ecstatic. I am sure we have turned the corner!

1 p.m. We head down to VEC for a rare Saturday examination and blood test with Kevin, as scheduled at our last appointment. Kevin does his usual thorough examination and then gives us some very bad news. All of Benjamin's lymph nodes are swollen. We are devastated. Kevin conducts blood tests, which come back within the acceptable range, gives Benjamin an injection of Benadryl, and, after a twenty minute wait, an unscheduled injection of chemo is administered.

As Benjamin is being treated, we speak with Kevin and I ask why we can't seem to get a handle on things. He explained that certain rogue cells are multiplying faster than the chemo can destroy them, and he tells us what I already know but never accepted — that the treatments will, over time, have less effect.

Tuesday, July 23, 6 p.m. The past two weeks have been the most trying of our lives. I have wanted to sit and continue to write this book, but we have been in an intense caregiving mode in addition to me of necessity having to get some work done.

On July 6, two days after Benjamin's additional chemo treatment, he had a violent reaction late at night, vomiting no less than six times and drinking huge amounts of water in between. We were anguished, distraught, worried in the extreme. The vomiting having stopped, he lay down weak and exhausted.

The next morning, I called VEC and asked to speak to a vet as neither Kevin nor an internist were in and Kevin wasn't expected back until the next day. My call was returned by Dr. Branka Grubor, an emergency room vet, an hour after her shift ended. She is kind, patient, and knowledgeable and diagnosed Benjamin's attack as tumour lysis syndrome, a potentially fatal condition whereby chemo causes cells to die so quickly they spill over into the body. Benjamin was quiet that morning, but Branka encouraged me to bring him in to get his electrolytes checked and prescribed some medication, which was waiting for us. I take Benjamin immediately, anxious because of the incident but also because I did not want to tax his energy any further — not to mention all of this is occurring during a massive sickening heat wave. We were greeted by the receptionist Reena and Benjamin was seen by Dr. Beth Lamborne, with assistance from animal technicians Beth and Vanessa and nurse Laura (who always baked special garlic-free cookies for Benjamin).

The days which followed saw Benjamin lying on the marble floor more than on his bed or even on the carpeting — often down the hall or by the elevator; in which case I sat down there and read or did some work. For the most part, though, Benjamin wanted to lie in the foyer of the building on the cool marble floor all hours of the day and night.

Many times a day, Benjamin needed to go out urgently, given a chronic case of diahrrea. On a few occasions, he bolted as soon as our door was open, ran down the hallway, and did his business at the far end of the hall. The stress for all of us was overwhelming. But more so, our hearts went out to our little boy. He was always so proud, that years earlier, staff at Tire Biter the doggie daycare, observed that Benjamin did not like to do his business in front of people and always tried to find a secluded spot to poo.

We have been out virtually every night in the middle of the night, sometimes more than once. Benjamin's appetite had also started to wane; he didn't want his canned food any longer.

On the afternoon of July 13, we rushed Benjamin back to the VEC to see Francesca, who is familiar with his case, having interned with Kevin a few months earlier. Benjamin's right eye is filling with 'guck' and we are increasingly alarmed. Francesca treats his eye, and gives us two ointments to apply five minutes apart starting later that evening. She also seems to suggest that we have done so much for our little boy and that we may be near the end.

I refuse to hear it. We continue to try everything we can in the food department, and thankfully, Benjamin polished off a bowl of freshly cooked extra lean ground beef. At different times, Benjamin has devoured pieces of freshly baked salmon, a scrambled egg, freshly cooked ground veal — we try anything and everything to make his food appealing and induce him to eat.

Sometimes sitting in the hallway late at night, or in the middle of it, I am hit by a wave of overwhelming emotion that things were not going well and that Benjamin won't make it. Sometimes this thought hits me when I am driving — and the tears flow. But then I say *No!* I am not going to let my little boy die! I am going to do everything in my power to make him well again.

The ride is like a rollercoaster. The incredible highs when Benjamin has eaten, come to the door to greet me, or more recently, got up and wagged his tail when he saw me coming down the hall on the days when I had to go out and was coming back from work. The walks we have had in the past few weeks, albeit much shorter — which I have attributed as much to his illness as to the warm weather. And the lows — when he didn't want to eat, was continually straining to do his business with ever-smaller amounts of loose elimination, when he wanted to lie in the hallway in the foyer of our building and I would sit down and doze a little there — fatigued in the extreme.

Helen has been increasingly worried these past weeks — for Benjamin, for me and for all of us. She worries desperately about him — she loves him with all her heart; and she worries that something will happen to me from months of not sleeping; working — or, at best, putting in long hours, much of which are completely unproductive; and fearing that if something were to happen to me such that I needed long-term care, our family unit will completely fall apart. And worried for herself, being on long-term disability with low grade chronic lymphocytic leukemia.

Cancer is such an insidious disease. It lies in wait, it stalks, it saps. It is evil.

The morning of July 15. I called our vet Dr. Bob to speak about our little boy. We are supposed to see Benjamin's oncologist Kevin at 12:40 p.m. that afternoon, and I wanted to talk about the advisability of further treatment given Benjamin's violent reaction the last time. I indicated to Bob that Helen and I didn't want to take Benjamin to VEC today. For many weeks now — really, since the start of this second round of chemo at the beginning of May, Benjamin has literally not wanted to go in the car. He is so smart, sensitive and intuitive; he has related the car to his treatments, which only just dawned on me. Helen told me several days ago that Benjamin had enough — and that he was trying to tell us. I didn't see it for what it was. I feel as if in his hour of need, I have failed him incredibly.

I told Bob that I wanted Helen and I to see Kevin that day without Benjamin to discuss treatment and the reality of his situation. Then, only if Kevin was firm on his conviction that another treatment would do it, would help Benjamin turn the corner, will we proceed. Bob agreed, and said that, at some point, a "decision" would need to be made. He explained that we all want our pets to crawl into bed with us and just drift off, but it usually doesn't work like that. And that while it is very painful to us, there comes a time when we have to give our little friend a helping hand — by making a decision for him which he can't make for himself.

This is the first time I hear these words. I have known this of course, but never in relation to Benjamin. I ask Bob on the phone through my tears, the most juvenile question — *"Why can't he just go on? Why does he have to go?"* My anguish is overwhelming; I feel so lost.

And Bob explains, as anyone would to a child, that in doggie years, Benjamin has had a very full, long and wonderful life that — as we all know, he has lived six and a half to seven human years for each of his. I thanked Bob sincerely for speaking with me.

I then called the VEC and left a message for Kevin that Helen and I would be coming in for our 12:40 p.m. appointment without Benjamin, for a consultation only. I had already called Barbara, our wonderful neighbour across the street, the night before, and arranged for her to stay with our little boy for an hour or so until we got back.

We went to see Kevin and explain Benjamin's deteriorating condition and asked for his thoughts. We were very distraught. Kevin, an exceptional oncologist, cool, unflappable, brilliant at what he does, talks about the insidious nature of cancer, which is always trying to outsmart the medication, and rendering the treatment options less and less effective and thereby reducing the number of treatments over time. He then steps out of the clinical role and explains that there comes a time when more treatment is not fair to Benjamin — that the whole point of treatment is not to prolong life forever, but to provide the highest quality of life as long as possible. What our role is as Benjamin's parents is to honour his life and how he has lived it and would want to still be living it — that honouring him was the most important thing we could do, even if the most painful.

Kevin was strong and eloquent, forceful but also incredibly sensitive. Helen and I are both in tears in front of Kevin and his intern, Dr. Launcelott. He doesn't rush, he doesn't try to usher us out. He gives us the time we need, and helps us come to terms with the reality of our baby boy's life and what the only option is left for us — the "decision" that Bob spoke to me about a few hours earlier.

Helen and I leave and are distraught. I drive her home and head to work, having a number of phone meetings booked in another time zone which will necessitate me working late — of all days.

Mercifully, I had the resolve this past weekend to cancel my trip out west, and book phone calls with several parties instead.

I got a call on my cell from Helen around 7:30 p.m., which I took in the midst of one of these phone conversations. She told me that Benjamin wasn't doing well — that he was lying in the lobby of our building and that, out of compassion and a desire to help, the concierge supervisor Pirahal carried him upstairs at one point; but that they were now back down again and Benjamin was just lying there. I promised to come home as soon as possible.

When I got home within the hour, I immediately went to the lobby and cradled Benjamin in my arms to take him upstairs. He lay down in the hallway of our apartment on the cool tile floor, and Helen and I talked. Benjamin hadn't eaten all day and didn't want anything that I tried to tempt him with. It was clear that he was suffering. I also saw his eyes, and they were so sad — not the brilliantly big clear bright eyes he had always had, but smaller and partially covered with residue.

We reflected on what Kevin had said, and came to the realization that we were near the end. We also knew that we didn't want Benjamin to experience a crisis in the middle of the night, necessitating a rush to emergency at the clinic in horrible trauma in a bright, sterile, hectic environment. At least we were at home.

I called Dr. Judy Brankolo, a palliative care vet referred to us by Drs. Bob and Bev at Eglinton Vet. I left her a message and she called back shortly. I am in tears, explaining Benjamin's current state and sharing with her my uncertainty and anguish. Judy suggested I monitor things and call her back in a little while. Helen and I talked some more, and resolved quickly to help our precious little boy to die with honour and dignity. I called Judy back, and she agreed to come within the hour.

Helen and I sat with Benjamin on the floor, and, remembering a suggestion from my friend Dave, I got the draft of this book and sat and read chapters from the first part to Benjamin and Helen — the day we first saw Benjamin at the OSPCA, the day we got him, our first trip to Montreal. I had my head on Benjamin's side and Helen was caressing him. It was peaceful but tinged with enormous sadness.

The phone rang. It was Andy, the concierge on duty, letting us know that Judy and her husband, who accompanies her on such visits, were here. I leave our front door open. A few minutes later Judy came in and Benjamin jumped up and let out a little bark. I was shocked, elated, and alarmed at the same time. How could I put my beloved dog down if he was still able to do that?

We talked to Judy, and Benjamin wanted to go outside into the hallway. No sooner had he left our apartment then he sat down right away. Judy was firm — he was very ill or that would never have happened. She used her stethoscope to listen to his heart and told us it was beating very fast — too fast for his own good. After a while, I urged Benjamin to come in and he lay down. Judy explained the procedure to follow — Helen and I listen but our hearts are broken and nothing is really registering. I pick Benjamin up and carried him to his little bed in our family room.

Then, Benjamin got up and wanted to go out again. I go down-stairs and he attempts to poo — although very strained. A very little bit came out and he then turned back towards the door. But he was too weak to walk and, this time, he let me pick him up and carry him back in. As I rode up in the elevator with him, his head was limp and I buried my face in his fur and cried. *"I love you Ben. I will always love you!"*

Even as I write the last part of this chapter one and a half weeks later, the tears stream down my face. The pain of losing my little boy is still too much to bear. (And as I dictated this for typing three weeks later, the tears still flowed.)

I put Benjamin down on his bed. He was standing up and very weak, and I gently got him to sit and gently pushed his front paws out so that he lay down. I moved him gently to the front of his favourite oval bed with a three inch high border, and he put his head on the rim. Judy and her husband have brought vanilla ice cream, to distract Benjamin while she injects the first of three solutions — the first one to tranquilize him completely, the second to anaesthetize and prevent pain, and the third to stop his heart. Judy tells me to give Benjamin some ice cream, but he refuses it. And then, having had a taste of a little bit on his lips, he instantly lifted his head and took three very quick licks off the spoon before resting his head on the rim of his bed for the very last time.

Within a very short period after the first injection, Benjamin was sleeping gently. We spent time with him talking to him and kissing his little head and still wet nose. Judy administered the second injection and then the third. She checked his heart for a beat in some six different places and tells us Benjamin is gone. Judy and her husband leave us alone for a while.

Helen and I are inconsolable. I cry out that I want him back. We tell him how much we love him. We tell him his suffering is now over.

At one point, Judy and her husband talked to us about arrangements for Benjamin, and we agreed to have him cremated at Gateway, a very reputable crematorium in Guelph, also home to the University of Guelph Veterinary College. We select a beautiful porcelain urn, and order two ceramic prints of Benjamin's front paw. We sign various forms. Judy's husband asks if Benjamin had a blanket he could wrap him in — I get Benjamin's favourite dark blue fleece, the one I would cover him with on a cold winter night, when he would curl up in a little ball on his big rectangular custom-made bed in our bedroom and tuck his head in tight to his body, shut his eyes tight, and let out a long sigh, surrendering himself to a blissful night's sleep after another great, active, fun-filled day. I also get Benjamin's two favourite toys — a little yellow squeaky duck and a little beige squeaky rabbit. We write Judy a cheque for her services, and she and her husband leave with Benjamin. Helen and I are left with our silence and grief.

Benjamin passed away just before midnight July 17, 2013.

At exactly the same time as my own father's passing
13 years less one month earlier.

He was approximately 14 ½.

Rainbow Bridge Poem

Just this side of heaven is a place called Rainbow Bridge.

When an animal dies that has been especially close to someone here, that pet goes to Rainbow Bridge.

There are meadows and hills for all our special friends so they can run and play together.

There is plenty of food, water and sunshine and our friends are warm and comfortable.

All the animals who have been ill and old are restored to health and vigour, those who were hurt or maimed are made whole and strong again, just as we remember them in our dreams of days and times gone by.

The animals are happy and content, except for one small thing; they each miss someone very special to them, who had to be left behind.

They all run and play together, but the day comes when one suddenly stops and looks in the distance. His bright eyes are intent. His eager body quivers. Suddenly he begins to run from the group, flying over the green grass, his legs carrying him faster and faster.

You have been spotted and when you and your special friend finally meet, you cling together in joyous reunion, never to be parted again. The happy kisses rain upon your face, your hands again caress the beloved head, and you look once more into the trusting eyes of your pet, so long gone from your life but never absent from your heart.

Then you cross Rainbow Bridge together...

Author unknown.

Epilogue

In life, the best walks are always too brief.

This sentiment was shared with us in a card from our friends and neighbours by Al and Maureen Bowbyes, in expressing their condolences on our loss.

Helen and I had 13 wonderful years with Benjamin. Never a day, never a minute of trouble did he cause — nothing but unconditional love from morning until night, sheer wonderment and joy, a love affair of love affairs.

And then it's over in a flash — your best friend, your little boy, the love of your life, is gone.

The apartment is quiet. Helen is very depressed, not eating, which is very bad for her given her health issues and being underweight to begin with. I have my work to occupy me during the days, and, as usual, to reside in the background and remind he how far behind I am all weekend. But Helen has nothing.

She shares a glimpse into just how intertwined hers and Benjamin's lives were — which I knew but never this clearly. I took Benjamin on his early morning walks, fed him breakfast, afterwards he would lie in the family room while I got ready for work, and then go and lie by Helen's bedside when I left. Helen tells me that, for the past seven years — since she went on long-term disability — Benjamin was the first 'person' she would speak to every morning; the one to share toast and cheese with while she had breakfast; the one to go on at least two if not three walks with including usually a very long one

94

at noon. They were inseparable, and the void in her life is like a deep wide chasm.

I reflect on how, regardless of what room you were in, Benjamin was there at your feet in no time. Whenever I sat down to eat, he was there with his head at my knee looking at me with his big ultra-bright brown eyes, wanting a nibble too. Rain or shine, sleet, snow or extreme heat, he had a two-hour biological clock built in and wanted to go out — and we indulged that and encouraged it from the very first day.

And now, to honour Benjamin and keep his memory and spirit alive, and to ensure we don't fall into a sad state of laziness and being out of shape, I go on a short walk every morning and we go on a long walk every night. And we carry Benjamin's collar with us every time.

We reminisce that every night, while we sat in the family room for a few minutes of TV — usually the nine o'clock national news followed by a re-run of Seinfeld, Benjamin would be on the couch curled up with Helen, would then move to the love seat just next to the couch and then over to the other love seat at the far end of the room where he slept like a log until he came to bed shortly after we did.

The night Benjamin passed away, there was an ultra fast pawing at my bedside at two different times in the middle of the night — about 10 times each occurrence. The first time I didn't get up — and have regretted it to this day. The second time I got up and opened the apartment door waiting for Benjamin to leave and come back in. On two other occasions since, Benjamin came to get me in the middle of the night and I actually went downstairs and outside for a few minutes. Think what you want, I know what I heard. I know he was there, and that he is there with us every minute of every day and night. His spirit and soul, his love and devotion.

We got Benjamin's remains back two days ago, and placed his beautiful urn on the mantle over our fireplace in the family room with his two paw prints, one on each side. I cry every morning and night at his little bed which is still in the family room; and now also at the urn as I place my hands around it.

Helen shares with me how Benjamin was her anchor. He sustained her all these years and gave her purpose. He filled the house with his presence. He was also the 'glue' that brought so many people together — the incredibly rambunctious and super-athletic doggie who got a whole group of dogs running around — and chasing him! in the park behind our home in the suburbs; and attracted so many peoples and dogs to him — and by extension to us — on a daily basis without exception in the city.

This sentiment, of Benjamin's unique qualities, which endeared him to so many people and other doggies, was reflected back to us by so many friends and neighbours in their kind words upon Benjamin's passing. Mary Ann, a lovely neighbour, drew a parallel between Benjamin and a Toronto resident of renown, David Rakoff, who also just passed away from lymphoma at the age of 46; and was, by every account, humble, simple, and someone who drew people to him in the best possible way. Indeed, according to a feature article on Mr. Rakoff upon his death, his parents were astounded by the outpouring of recognition and affection, so unassuming was he in life.

"Sometimes our lives are touched by gentle friends who stay only for awhile... but remain forever in our hearts.."
Anonymous

For many months, we have been scheduled to go on vacation — the three of us of course — to our favourite place in the Mont Tremblant area of the Laurentians. Our departure date is next weekend. We both need to get away, and I don't have any idea how, given how far behind I am in my work. And, neither of us feel like going anywhere, we are so saddened by our loss.

Helen wonders if Benjamin got sick to take the burden of cancer off of her and save her. Benjamin was in such a league of his own — in caring, compassion sensitivity, intellect, and, of course, athleticism. I have never thought of this before, but I wouldn't be surprised. Benjamin would have given his life for us, and maybe he did.

I recall a conversation I had several months ago with a friend and colleague, Christine. I was late for a 9 a.m. meeting with her, having walked Benjamin — I believe it may have been the second walk that morning. I told Christine about him and The Benjamin Project — not something I would typically do in a business context, but I did.

Christine was exceptional in her empathy, understanding and insight. She shared with me that dogs are such special creatures — they live in the moment; they don't filter anything the way we do. They don't construct a socially accepted story about reality the way we do either — every action is real just as it unfolds: no manipulations, no pretentions. They are child-like in nature. Our distorted and false pride leads us to think we are superior to other species. We impose our egocentric way of thinking on the planet — and look what that begets. Dogs just want to embrace every living creature as a friend, and make everything and everyone around them happy.

It seems hardly a day goes by at this point where there isn't an article, a news clip on TV, or a major program such as the one on The Passionate Eye last night (August 12, 2013) profiling the amazing attributes of dogs and their incredible loving relationship with people. Within the past week alone, there was a news clip about The Horse Boy Project, a program in Nova Scotia which places young autistic children in very close proximity to beautiful gentle horses and has a transformative healing impact on their lives. Another article, which appeared in the Toronto Star July 20, 2013 entitled "Healing Horsepower", profiled a program for people of all ages to help overcome a long list of mental health issues in an emerging field called equine-assisted therapy and learning. The specific program, HEAL with Horses, is one of several in Ontario and is part of a worldwide phenomenon.

Along these same lines, a two-page article in the August 3, 2013 edition of the Globe and Mail entitled *"Who needs whom?"* by John Allemang, offered the following:

"...Dogs have been domesticated for roughly 30,000 years, and cats for around 10,000 but only recently has power shifted in their favour. The creatures who were once our labourers and our servants, those hangers-on who guarded flocks or rid settlements of vermin in exchange for human protection and rarely saw the inside of a house or the warmth of a smile, now share and shape our lives.

....Now the number of pets has risen above 14 million in Canada, and our animals have become more of our human equivalents to be talked to and fussed over, family members who are loved in life and mourned in death. Their elevated status and newfound styles of behaviour would astonish our harder-hearted ancestors.

Just don't dare to suggest that all this fawning over our pets is ultimately a form of narcissism, an attention-getting device where we lavish inappropriate feelings on creatures who are designed by evolution and breeding to throw it right back at us — even as we diminish the status of other intelligent animals who administer to our carnivorous needs.

We are, after all, part of an unparalleled moment in domestic-animal history, as demographics shift in parallel with societal norms to support a new kind of pet-owner relationship. In this sluggish economy, the households shrink in size, and mobile families have naturally grown more disconnected — are we likely to feel closer to a sister on the other side of the country that you glimpse once a year at best (or worst), or the dog who is always there when you are?

...To make sense of this, just read the daily death announcement where faithful pets now occupy pride of place among the bereaved. Or contemplate a study that revealed the health-giving aspect of an old person's pooch; dog owners who have had heart surgery are more likely to get up sooner and take their canine companion for a walk. Animals give us a purpose, a sense of meaning, and an altruistic obligation to be active and aware.

Younger people know this as well. Whether because they don't trust an uncertain economy that prizes short-term contracts and lower-wage jobs, or because they resist the existing models of maturity and adulthood, they're putting off marriage, children, and other lifelong commitments. Once again, that leaves pets as emotional substitutes, as a way to overrule the world's disappointments.

...Our pets supply a loyalty that is hard to find in a downsized economy; they don't judge us or leave us for someone younger or gossip about us behind our backs.

They're used more and more in therapy situations because of their wide-ranging affection — they don't feel our need to make superficial distinctions between pretty and plain, mobile and disabled, self-assertive and shy.

Dogs and cats are also much more comfortable than humans with prolonged eye contact. Anyone can look into their eyes and get something back.

"The eyes are called the windows into the soul for a very good reason," Michael Meehan, who teaches at the Ontario Veterinary College at the University of Guelph, says, "There's very strong evidence that when we stare into someone's eyes for a period of time, everything else dissipates and we feel a strong connection.""

After a lot of anguish and dissonance, Helen and I headed up to our remote spot in the Laurentians a week ago, three weeks after Benjamin's passing. We are exhausted and worried that the memories of the wonderful times we spent here with Benjamin over the years would be too painful. But I had booked this secluded house on a hill overlooking a pristine lake back in January, and had pinned so much hope on all of us coming here together; and we desperately needed to get away for awhile. I couldn't imagine going anywhere else, getting into a busy mode in another environment. The peace and tranquility of this place is proving to be just what we need after all.

Several times since we arrived, Benjamin has awoken me in the middle of the night to go out — as he did on occasion in this same house in years gone by, long before his illness. Sometimes, it's a pawing at my bedside; on two occasions, my "wake-up call" has been a very loud clattering coming from the wall just outside the bedroom — not the pitter-patter of mice or other creatures! Again, you can say whatever you wish — I know what I heard each time. I got up and let Benjamin out, and then we both went back to sleep.

I carry Benjamin's collar with me everywhere, and the handwritten manuscript of the new parts of this book that I am completing up here. Helen wonders if carrying his collar is preventing Benjamin from moving on to a better place — keeping his soul a prisoner of my grief and desperate attachment. But I feel differently.

I have gotten back to mediating here, twice a day. And in my meditation, I send love and light to Benjamin and pray this is liberating, while telling him that we are always together. For me, there is no conflict, and I pray I am right. As I sit here on the porch, looking out at a forest through which I can see the lake down below — a very gentle current rippling across an otherwise mirror-like surface — Helen is writing acknowledgement cards to close to a hundred people who have sent beautiful messages of condolence to us and several donations in Benjamin's memory.

It is remarkable how many have reflected on Benjamin's character — his wisdom, his gentle nature, his friendliness and beauty; and how many referred to him as "a real person". In our darkest moments, it is somewhat comforting to read their sentiments about us having given Benjamin the best life a doggie could have ever had.

Of course, this is all small consolation. Oh, to be able to trade it in for a split second to have Benjamin back. But, it is sincere and well intentioned, and something we *must* internalize. Thinking about the end only is far too distressing.

I reflect, though, how easy it could be to just "move on" or "passed" one's grief. You get busy at work, go off on a holiday, "get on with life" — as I did when my father passed away, or other family members. And before you know it, there are meaningful albeit infrequent reflections, hopefully good, and life carries on. It is undoubtedly normal and healthy. But I am committed to more, much more, this time. Benjamin was my best friend, and the centre of my and Helen's lives. A bundle of wisdom, goodness, and joy. I will embrace him deeply forever, cry for him, smile for him, and more importantly, try to honour him every day of my life.

Benjamin was a gift to me from Helen. But he was also a gift to the world. Helen and I often reflect on the unbelievable circumstances which led her — and us, to him at that very moment in time, to that very cage he was in, on that very beautiful warm spring day in May, 13 years ago. And, on how he came into the right family — the one which indulged him, thrived on his two-hour built in wanting-to-go-out 'clock', doted on him, smothered him with love, and got so much more in return. And, as sad as we are, we are also proud that we gave him a sense of security and wellbeing — so that he could have the best life possible, that he so richly deserved.

Go play with doggie, doggie, doggies, my baby boo-boo. We are always together, even as we are apart, and one day we will all be completely together again.

I love you, Ben.

Dealing with the illness of your pet (or any loved one) isn't easy. The anxiety can be overwhelming, because the uncertainty is so great. Not to mention that watching a pet experiencing illness is very distressing. And I am not even referring to what might be the outcome. I'm talking about what is actually happening to your precious baby boy or girl at the time. What stage is the illness at? Will it arrest, or, ideally, reverse? Is this the best treatment? Is diahrrea really just a side effect of medication or an indication of something more? And, perhaps most anxiety provoking of all, what can you do to get your pet to eat if he or she has stopped? The list goes on. And the truth is, for some of these questions there are no ready answers, if any.

A few thoughts which are hopefully helpful. Trust your vet (or change). Ask any and all questions. Yes, doctors can be intimidating, but you MUST advocate for your beloved pet and you need to understand as much as you can about whatever is occurring. Research to the extent that you can, but recognize also that some — perhaps much — of what you find on the Internet or elsewhere may not apply to your pet's condition and may even be misleading. Listen to your pet! If he or she is, all of a sudden, running out of the groomers or the clinic, or doesn't want to go in the first place, he is telling you something very clearly. He is not being difficult! If he doesn't want to get in the car, but had readily jumped in in the past, he is telling you something! You have to figure out what and then what to do about it. But he is not just 'acting out'.

Last, 'check under the hood'. Ask the groomer how they go about things. TELL THEM if your pet is afraid of water. TELL THEM you do not want your pet on a two-inch chain while being washed, scrubbed overly strenuously; or otherwise stressed out. QUALIFY a dog walker. Check references; find out about the routine; ask if they ever leave the dogs in their charge unattended — for example, in an SUV while going into someone's home or apartment to pick up the next dog on the route. SPEAK UP — as tactfully as possible to someone you know, perhaps more forcefully if you don't if you see a case of abuse or something more innocent but still concerning, such as keeping a dog tied up on the sidewalk on a hot sunny day while its owner is having a coffee; or seeing an unpleasant encounter between a well known aggressive animal in your neighbourhood and an unfortunate one who is the latest innocent victim.

I am mindful that likely the vast majority of pet owners love their pet as much as we loved Benjamin, and that some of these seemingly mundane activities are necessary and undertaken with the best of intentions. Don't drive yourself crazy over them. Just be informed, and then legitimately feel good about things — you are doing your best, and that's all anyone can do.

Acknowledgments

In addition to those mentioned throughout the book, I would like to thank the following people for their help and encouragement in making this 'labour of love' a reality:

Holger Kluge, for his insights into The Benjamin Project, review of the draft, generosity, and powerful suggestion to incorporate small inserts of an educational nature throughout the book;

Dave Slapack, for his several reviews of the draft, great edits, thoughts on publicizing the book, and his unequivocal enthusiasm and support;

David Shaul, for five great photos, his affection for Benjamin, and his commitment to The Benjamin Project;

Holger Kluge, for his insights into The Benjamin Project, review of the draft, and powerful suggestion to incorporate small inserts of an educational nature throughout the book;

Ceilidh Marlow (Author Account Manager), Matt Robitaille (Publishing Consultant), Mary Metcalfe (Editor), and Shay Kuhnert (Book Designer), at FriesenPress for their invaluable assistance and support; and Mary for her beautiful testimonial;

Sharon Laughlin and Jennifer Cummings, for their wonderful typing assistance, and Jennifer for her great graphics;

Nira Kolers, for her time to read the draft and her unreserved enthusiasm;

Christine Forsyth, for her reflections and wisdom;

Laura and Nolan Machan, for their great ideas on publicity;

Sherry and Ben D'Costa, for their wonderful assistance with marketing and distribution;

Don Tapscott, for his insights and referrals for website design and publicity;

James Christopher, Steve Litwin, Sylvia Lowndes, and Dave Wallace for their kind assistance;

George Sallay, for his ongoing support, empathy, and understanding;

Wendy Korentager, for her significant insights into The Benjamin Project concept;

Yvonne Charbonneau, for her articles, invaluable information, and prayers;

Brenda Bickram and Art Sandler, respectively, for their generosity and support;

Dave Marshall, for his review of the draft, suggestions, and inspiring testimonial;

Jeffrey Masson, for his immediate response to my email on New Year's Day 2014 and gracious testimonial;

Peter and Alison George, for their caring and genuine support;

The wonderful staff and residents in our building, who loved Benjamin and were so kind and considerate to the three of us;

I know I have already mentioned the following people, but heartfelt thanks again to Dr. Bob Watson and his colleagues at Eglinton Veterinary Facilities, for their years of the best medical care; Dr. Kevin Finora and colleagues at Veterinary Emergency Clinic, for their expertise and professionalism; Dr. Jaime Modiano at the School of Veterinary Medicine and Masonic Cancer Center, University of Minnesota, for his incredible responsiveness and compassion;

Diane, Keith, Louise, Roland and pooches for their enthusiasm and great support;

Barbara Chudy, Jennifer Cummings, Janice Ingram, and Sharon Laughlin for their trusted loving "babysitting," and Barbara for her kind help with sales and marketing; our neighbours Lynne Fingold, the late Aliza and her husband Chaim Lustig, and the late Mr. Gray for their love and treats — I know these made Benjamin's day as did his exciting visits to your suites make yours; and Allison Burgess, Benjamin's wonderful sitter on those few occasions earlier on when Helen and I went away for a week, and Benjamin's named 'guardian' in the event anything ever happened to Helen and me;

Judith Bennatar, for her generosity of spirit, thoughtfulness, and exquisite boots, and Timber for his enduring friendship with Benjamin;

Lori Pumputis of Kitty Cat Rescue, for her review of the draft, offer of assistance, and incredible voluntary work;

Janice Ingram, for her wonderful support and great work with rescues;

Dorothy Sjogren, Pamela Pua, Paul Daniels and the team at The Printing House for their generous support of The Benjamin Project, great design work, and affection for Benjamin on his many visits to the branch;

Nina and Jeff Lewin and Maddy, for their enthusiasm and support;

Paul Waldie of The Globe and Mail, for his wonderful article on The Benjamin Project; his colleagues Fred Lum, photographer, Theresa Suzuki, Assistant Photo Editor, and Barbara Smith of the reference team;

Lynne Kurylo, for her kind referral on website design, and Dave Barr for his great website;

Ken Jewett, for his insights on establishing The Benjamin Project framework;

Karen Cho, Karen Devlin, and Laura Hiscock at St. Clair Greetings for their affection for Benjamin, and to Karen Cho for selling this book;

Ann Rohmer, host of CP 24's Animal House Calls, for her unabashed enthusiasm and wonderful publicity;

Heather Payne of HackerYou for her ideas and referrals for website design;

Joe Drantz and Lucy, for their encouragement and loving thoughts;

Dr. Karen Nasir, for her great help on strategy for The Benjamin Project

Jacques Messier, CEO, Barbara Steinhoff, Executive Director, and the Board of the Toronto Humane Society, for their gracious and invaluable support; Linda McKinnon, Judi King, and Jason Peetsma for their unabashed enthusiasm; and Norman, a big rambunctious Bouvier at THS, for being part of the Globe and Mail photo and making our day;

Margaret Peppler, for her devotion to animals and commitment to perpetuating the ideals such as are in The Benjamin Project through her own writings;

Jordan Struminikovski at Bank of Montreal, for his prompt and professional assistance in opening up The Benajmin Project account for donations;

Michelle Fortnum for her enthusiastic support and her best friend Senji, who loved Benjamin and now romps with him;

The many friends, acquaintances and colleagues, whose kindness and empathy sustained us when we needed it most;

Diane, Keith, Brandy and Minnie, and Louise, Roland and Dunzee, for their love, support and passionate belief in The Benjamin Project;

My cousins Myra, Rich and Fern, Rich's wife Mimi, and first cousin once removed Jenny, for their support and website ideas;

My sister Nancy, for her love of Benjamin.

My mother Elsie, who asks about Benji every day of the year;

Last, to my wife Helen: Thank you for giving me the greatest gift imaginable, by bringing Benjamin into our lives.

Dog had his day — now his story is helping other shelter pets

By PAUL WALDIE

Malcolm Bernstein's diary of family terrier Benjamin touches on range of animal welfare issues

The donors: Malcolm Bernstein and Helen Brent

The gift: Raising at least $100,000

The cause: Animal shelters and welfare organizations

When Helen Brent gave her husband a terrier for his 50th birthday, the little dog quickly became an integral part of their family.

Over the years, Mr. Bernstein began jotting down notes about their life with Benjamin and it eventually became something of a diary. When Benjamin died last summer after a long illness, Mr. Bernstein turned his notes into The Benjamin Project, a book and companion educational package that touches on a wide range of animal welfare issues, including how to care for a seriously ill pet, tips on feeding and travelling, and what children need to know about caring for animals.

"It's a book aimed at pet owners," said Mr. Bernstein, now 63, who is an executive recruiter in Toronto and also volunteers with the Toronto Humane Society. Ms. Brent has retired from working in the non-profit sector.

The pair plan to launch the project this spring and all proceeds from the sale of the book and other items will go to animal welfare charities. Their goal is to raise at least $100,000 and introduce the project to schools across Ontario.

The couple haven't gotten another dog and aren't sure they ever will. "He took over our lives," Mr. Bernstein said. "He brought such unbelievable joy to so many people. ... [The project] is for all the Benjamins out there."

Animals and Their Legal Rights

"We owe ourselves the duty not to be brutal or cruel; and we owe to God the duty of treating all of His creatures according to His own perfections of love and mercy."
Cardinal Henry E. Manning July 13, 1891

The voices began to clamour in the 1700's among English-speaking peoples for animal protection legislation. Jeremy Bentham's book, *An Introduction to the Principles of Morals and Legislation*, first published in 1780, is regarded as a classic by law students today. In his book, Bentham argues realistically in defence of animals' rights at the same time he is arguing realistically in defence of human rights. In an astonishingly advanced line of reasoning considering that the year is 1780, he asks, "The question is not, *Can they reason? nor Can they talk? but, Can they suffer?"*

Lord Erskine introduced a bill for the prevention of cruelty to animals into the House of Lords in England on May 15, 1809. The bill was passed by the Lords but lost in the Commons by 37 to 27, thereby falling to the lot of an Irishman, Richard Martin (1754-1834), to succeed in bringing the first English legislation to passage. Widely known for his love of animals, "Humanity Martin" as he was called by his personal friend, King George IV, was not only human but also practical. He consulted a well-known expert John Lawrence, to help him on the details of his bill. Lawrence (1753-1839), described as a literary farmer, was an authority on agriculture and the management of domestic animals. From the alliance of these two humanitarians,

111

Martin and Lawrence, came forth the first legislation in England for the prevention of cruelty to animals.

Lawrence was the humanitarian who wrote the following in *A Philosophical Treatise on Horses and on the Moral Duties of Man Towards the Brute Creation*:

> "Justice, in which are included mercy and compassion, obviously refers to sense and feeling. Now is the essence of justice divisible? Can there be one kind of justice for men, and another for brutes? Or is feeling in them a different thing to what it is in ourselves? Is not a beast produced by the same rule, in the same order of generation with ourselves? Is not his body nourished by the same food, hurt by the same injuries; his mind actuated by the same passions and affections which animate the human breast; and does not he, also, at last, mingle his dust with ours, and in like manner surrender up the vital spark to the aggregate, or fountain of intelligence? Is his spark, or soul, to perish because it chanced to belong to a beast? Is it to be annihilated? Tell me, learned philosophers, how that may possibly happen."

America has the distinction of being the first country to acknowledge the rights of animals by enacting statutory legislation to protect them from cruel treatment. In 1641, the Puritans of the Massachusetts Bay Colony voted to have printed their first legal code, "The Body of Liberties". Liberty 92 of the 100 "liberties" the Puritans expected to enjoy and observe, was: Cruelty to Animals forbidden.

As far as can be determined, the first anti-cruelty law among the United States was enacted in 1828 by the New York State Legislature.

By 1866, when Henry Bergh secured legislative consent for the incorporation of the American Society for the Prevention of Cruelty to Animals, 20 states had enacted anti-cruelty laws. Bergh's real masterpiece of legal draftsmanship came in 1867 when *An Act for the More Effectual Prevention of Cruelty to Animals* was passed April 12, and has since served as the example for the drafting of many succeeding anti-cruelty laws throughout the United States.

Source: Animal Welfare Institute

"The indifference, callousness and contempt that so many people exhibit toward animals is evil first because it results in great suffering in animals, and second because it results in an incalculably great impoverishment of the human spirit."

Ashley Montague

Benjamin's Meds

Medication	Amount	Time	Check mark
Fortiflora	1 packet per day	Breakfast	
Prednisone	3 tablets per day	8 pm	
Salmon oil	⅕ teaspoon	Lunch	
Nausea-Metoclopramide	1 tablet twice a day – every 12 hours only if needed	10:30 am 10:30 pm **note:** every 12 hours	
Diarrhea-Metronidazole	¾ tablet twice a day - every 12 hours only if needed	8 am 8 pm **note:** every 12 hours	
Diarrhea - Tylosin	1 tablet twice a day – every 12 hours only if needed	10:30 am 10:30 pm **note:** every 12 hours	
Liver pill-Ursodiol	1 pill per day	supper	

GIVE A CARROT IN THE AFTERNOON!!!

A Heartwarming Exchange with Bob

From: Bob
To: Malcolm
Sent: July 7, 2013 10:58 AM
Hi Malcolm,

I am sorry to hear that Benjamin is not doing well. It is most important that he stays hydrated, otherwise he may have to go on IV fluids to keep up his strength.

When I talked to Helen at the end of this week, she told me that Benjamin was not even interested in her chicken burgers. Even if you can hand feed him some of the I/d or even chicken broth so he is getting some nutrients and energy.

He also may need some injectable medication like Pepsid (famotidine) to relieve the vomiting.

Keep us posted on Benjamin's progress and give him a pat for us.
Dr. Bob

—

From: Malcolm
To: Bob
Sent: July 7, 2013 7:36 PM
Bob,

PS A breakthrough tonight! Benjamin ate a big homemade chicken burger for the first time in weeks! (also a scrambled egg this aft!– he didn't want his meat)

A big paw from Benj.
Malcolm and Helen

—

From: Bob
To: Malcolm
Sent: July 7, 2013 7:36 PM
Thanks for the update. I always told Benjamin that Helen was a great cook.
Have a good night.
Dr Bob

E-Mails and Cards

Dear Malcolm and Helen,

We were so saddened to hear about Benjamin. He seemed like such a wonderful dog, and we know how important he was to you both. He truly was lucky to have been part of your family and to have had such a good life.

With deep sympathy for your loss,

Myra and Bill

—

Dear Helen and Malcolm

I am truly sad to hear about Benjamin. He was a favourite model for my camera. Although you have lost him, remember the wonderful times you had with him

David

—

I am so terribly sorry you have lost your boy. He was lovely....my thoughts are with you both at this most difficult time.

Karen

—

Oh Malcolm. I am so deeply saddened by your news. How is it that I asked yesterday instead of a month or two ago. I feel very badly about that. You were such an amazing dad and he will be smiling down on you. My very heartfelt condolences. He is at peace. You must know that.

Rita

—

Dear Malcolm,

I was dismayed to hear that Benjamin had passed away. From what I know of the feelings of warmth and caring that he evoked in you and others this was truly a very special being. His passing does cause one to reflect on what is truly important in life.

Warmest regards

Paul

—

Oh dear, Malcolm, this is so sad. I know you were devoted to Benjamin and he to you. This is very, very hard…my heart goes out to you.

Take care of yourself too…

Virginia

—

Dear Helen and Malcolm,

We're so sorry for your loss. Benjamin was such a good dog and a precious friend. We know that he cannot be replaced and we are very sad. He will remain in our hearts. Our thoughts are with you. Please tell us if we can do anything to help.

Love

Louise, Roland and Dunzee

—

Hi Malcolm

I am so sorry for your loss. Benjamin was a wonderful pup and I know how much I will miss ours when the time comes.

My thoughts are with you and Helen at this difficult and sad time.

Please take care.
Dave

—

Our deepest sympathy to both of you. May you treasure the memories of Benjamin, his friendship and unconditional love forever.
Claudette and Holger

—

M — my heart goes out to you and Helen. You paint a wonderful picture of Benjamin below.
Please let me know how I can help — a listening ear, a coffee.....
My thoughts are with you,
Brad

—

Malcolm, Very sad, my thoughts are with you.
Jack

—

Malcolm, so sorry to hear about Benjamin; I know you were very close to him.
I lost my first dog when I was in Grade 6 and I couldn't go to school for days.
My heartfelt condolences.
Sal

—

Dear Helen and Malcolm. How truly sorry I am to learn of Benjamin's passing. I so appreciate how much Benjamin meant, over 13 years, to you both and how integral he was in your daily lives. He was undoubtedly a loving and beloved member of the Bernstein family and by all accounts he knew that.

May you find comfort and support from one another and from your friends, particularly in your neighborhood and in the nearby park, who share your grief.

Big hugs to you both,

Janice

—

Dear Malcolm and Helen,

Colette and I are extremely sad to learn of Benji's passing. He was the most wonderful and unique dog with his own personality. He certainly was the boss as we could see when walking was concerned. Benji lived a great life and had the best of care with parents such as you. We know that this is a great loss but Benji returned your love in many countless ways. He was one in a million!!!

We hope to see you on the street and maybe you will maybe find a second Benji in due course, with kind regards,

Brian and Colette

—

Oh Malcolm, I can hardly see through my tears to type a response to this news. I know all too well the pain you and Helen are currently experiencing and wish there were some words I could offer to ease your heartache. Frankly, there are none. Benjamin was a wonderful dog and companion to you both, and he knew he was loved beyond measure. He was your connection to the neighbourhood and as such will be missed by so many of us who liked nothing better than to stop, say hello to you both while giving him a friendly pat and a rub behind the ears.

Please do try to take some measure of comfort in knowing he is now free from his struggle. In time you may feel able to read a piece of poetic prose called "Rainbow Bridge". It gives me hope there is such a place where we may see our beloved pets again.

My thoughts are with you both at this very difficult time.

Warm regards,

Dale

—

Hi Malcolm,

I am very sorry to hear, and I cannot imagine how painful this must be. He was the luckiest dog to have you and Helen take him into your home when he was homeless, then give him the best possible doggie life any dog could hope for.

It was a pleasure to know and help care for Ben, and I will always remember what a neat boy he was. I was always amused by the attention he attracted on our walks, he inspired much curiosity in people!

Be at peace knowing he lived a very long and full life. You will always have the wonderful memories of the years you shared together.

Take care, and thinking of you,

Janice

—

Hi Helen and Malcolm

I just heard from Ricki that Benjamin is in Doggie heaven.

I am so sad for the both of you and know how difficult a time this is. Your hearts have been ripped in half with the loss of this amazing duman.. Dog human!

He was more human than dog. Just cherish all the memories and hope to see you walking.

With love

Jacquie and Yankee

—

Hello Malcolm,

I've just heard about your very sad news....I'm so sorry!! I know how hard it is to lose a beloved pet — I still mourn Maggie whom we lost nearly 7 years ago — despite having another fantastic dog! They become such a special part of the family and their absence is so sorely felt.

I hope you keep well. You are in my thoughts!

Sue

—

Hi Helen and Malcolm,

I was so sorry to hear about Benjamin. I was away from the city for the past 3+ weeks, and got back only late last night. Heard from Pirahal this morning about Benjamin passing away and felt so sad. Sad for him, and even sadder for you who loved, and still love, him so much. I can imagine how acute your pain is, and I know the grief and mourning will go on for a long time. But I also know that the joy he gave you, and the effects of the special and beautiful relationship you had with him will be part of you for ever. A lasting gift.. And by the same token, the love and attention you always showered on him gave his life a richness and uniqueness that are uncommon; and that your connection to him also shaped the way he was: kind and wise and high spirited and loving.

Thank you for your note about Benjamin, and for sharing your thoughts and feelings.

I know Benjamin will rest in peace, and I know he will live in your loving memories for ever. I also know that all who knew Benjamin had a special feeling for him as he endeared himself so naturally and so easily. In our own way, we all share in the sadness.

Nira

—

Malcolm,

I am so sorry to hear this sad news. I do know the valiant effort Benjamin showed as he faced several health challenges along the way. I know too of the many wonderful memories you and Helen will have of all the time you enjoyed with Benjamin as you progress beyond this very sad time.

So sorry

Jack

—

—

Dear Malcolm + Helen :

I was so sorry to hear about the passing of Ben. He was an institution here and the mascot for the building.

He was the only dog in the building with whom I identified and whose name I always remembered!

My dog, Coco, died three years ago, and I too know what it means to lose a "member of the family".

I am enclosing two articles which I hope might give you some solace in your grief.

I would also like you to know that a memorial donation is being sent to the Pet Trust at Guelph Vet. College in Ben's name. You have all my sympathy & anything I can do to help you!

Mary Ann

—

Good morning Malcolm;

I am so sorry to hear about Benjamin; I know how much he meant to you.

We can certainly set up a fund for him to honor his memory.

I am away next week for a week of holiday.

Let me know of your availability the following week and we can get together and discuss how we can make this happen.

Once again I am so sorry for your loss.

Jacques

—

Just picked up your note for which I thank you........

Will pop in sometime tomorrow — will call first

I too am so sad — but what a gorgeous photo — David really captured the warmth in his eyes and that very special look he gave us all

He will be sorely missed

Love Pauline XX

—

Dear Helen and Malcolm

I was so distraught to receive the email from Meaghan regarding Benjamin's passing. As much as you try to prepare yourself for the eventuality, it is another matter once it arrives. Our hearts go out to you both, as we understand what you are going through. The pain will surely pass, but the loving memories will last forever.

Eric and Garian

—

Dear Helen and Malcolm:

We are so sorry to learn of Benjamin's passing. We know how much you all meant to each other, and we know what you're going through.

Keep his memories near and dear.

Love,

Debby and Barry

—

Dear Malcolm, Helen & Benjamin,

I have been grieving since I read your note. Benjamin was your Best Friend and you were certainly his Best Friends. He gave all he could to both of you. And you gave back that same love. I know you are in terrible pain, but I believe we're so much richer because of your loving boy. He could not have had a better Mom and Dad. I believe his spirit is still with you. That much love and energy does not go away. I am sharing this note with Lucy and Jeff.

Love,

Joe

—

Malcolm,

I read this and wanted you to know how special even Alex Colville knew your "boy" was. Alex Colville the Canadian artist spoke in Toronto 20 years ago taking special pains to explain his interest in his family's pets. His interest in these subjects is rooted in his curiosity about the human species.....and referring to his pets:

'They are angels in our midst, pure goodness, without guile, without vengeance or malice or pride, attentive and capable of selfless love in ways that we can (as humans) only aspire to. Their example underscores the complexity and darkness of our own natures'. This must be a very tough weekend.

Take care, Jack

—

Malcolm and Helen –
We are so sorry for your loss. I think we understand having had similar experiences. Our thoughts are with you.

Doug and Barbara

—

Omg just heard your sad news, I'm so very sorry for you all, what a devastating loss. We understand your pain. Was just looking at my two lying on the sofa with me watching the British Open, on their backs, knowing they can be in such a vulnerable position because they are so loved, totally relaxed, and thinking what great company they are to me, especially when Doug is away. From everything you have told me in the past Benjamin was such a wonderful boy. Be happy knowing you gave him a wonderful life and he loved you the same. There are so many out there that don't have what our dogs do, homes where they are safe and so very much a part of the family. You gave him the best, and he gave you his. You will always have those wonderful memories. Thinking of you today.

Barbie

—

Malcolm, it is very difficult to lose a loved one. My thoughts are with you.

All the best
Brian

—

Hi Malcolm
I just heard the sad news! I am so sorry!
I will keep you all in my thoughts and prayers!
Anna

—

Malcolm, Helen,
Jill and I are very saddened to hear this news. Our thoughts are with you.
Kevin & Jill

—

Hello Helen & Malcolm,
My heart dropped before I even opened this email as something told me what the news was going to be. Somehow I knew it was that the most loving, kind, amazing boy Benjamin had passed. I am so sorry to hear such incredibly sad news. Benjamin will be missed so dearly as he was so well loved and such a unique boy. I have never met a dog like Benjamin. All my memories of him warm my heart as they are full of nothing but happy, silly times. You two are the kindest, most caring pet owners I have ever known. I know you were incredibly lucky to have Benjamin as he was perfect, however he was very lucky too. I am so very sorry for your loss, I know you must be hurting a lot right now. My thoughts are with you, I will miss Benjamin terribly. May you find comfort in the amazing life you provided for him.
Allison

—

Dear Helen and Malcolm
We are so sorry to hear the news about Benjamin. We hope the good memories will endure and help overcome the grief. He was a lucky guy to have people like you in his life to care for him and provide the best possible quality of life a pup could ever have.

Please accept our deepest, most sincere sympathy.
The Modiano Lab
College of Veterinary Medicine and Masonic Cancer Center
University of Minnesota

—

Hi Helen and Malcolm,
Rhona, Joanne and Mike are currently on vacation on the west coast coming back Sunday night.
We are extremely sorry and sad to hear about this huge loss to both of you. Benjamin was like a son to you. We do not know anyone who took a better care of their pet than both of you. The way he related to you it is beyond words to describe.
We wish you strength in this difficult time.
Rhona, George, Joanne and Mike

—

Helen and Malcolm
We are very sorry for you in your loss.
Like yourselves, we had a special dog in our lives. The emptiness does fade but the memory never does. Myra was visiting last week and we were sharing stories of our great dogs. The conversation grew to include Benjamin and the both of you. Your places are secure in the land of legends relative to people-dog relationships. It takes a Jewish person from Montreal to find the words.
Leonard Cohen in his song/poem "Everybody knows"
"Everybody knows that the boat is leaking
Everybody knows that the captain lied
Everybody got this broken feeling
Like their father or their dog just died"

Best wishes
Mimi and Rich

—

Dear Malcolm,

I'm sorry to hear that your time with Benjamin has come to an end. Based on everything you told me about Benjamin, he was an amazing dog. I hope you find some comfort in knowing that he lived a full and wonderful life under your care. I hope in time, another animal will be so lucky to be accepted into your hearts.

Wishing you and Helen comfort and strength at this difficult time.

Tanya

—

Malcolm,

I wanted to pass along my sincere condolences on the recent passing of your beloved Benji. Letting go of our four-legged family members is never an easy task, even when it is something that we must face.

Rest assured that you and your wife gave him a wonderful life and that he will always watch over the two of you from heaven.

All the best,

Lara

—

Dear Malcolm and Helen,

Just got your message about Benjamin. I am deeply sorry to hear of your loss and share in your pain. Our fur family is indeed beloved. Benjamin and you both shared so much together; he was the most loved dog ever. Healing of sorrow takes time and leaves us with memories of comfort.

I'm in Minneapolis with Arielle and Ryan and will call you when I get back to Ottawa on the 13th. Meantime, please know I am thinking of you both and sending you lots of hugs and caring.

From all of us,

Love,

Fern

—

Please get to the healing of the mountains as soon as you can, and do what you need to honour Benjamin. He would have loved this upcoming trip with you and would want to have frolicked in nature till he snored. Good memories keep us going. Give yourselves all the time you need to grieve and remember your boy.

Thinking of you both and send you lots of love,

Fern

—

Hi Malcolm and Helen,

Thank you for your very kind letter. Taking care of Benjamin overnight was such a pleasure and I'm grateful I had many opportunities to do so. I appreciated your trust always and Benjamin was such a blessing to care for. I'm sure the pain is still very deep for the both of you and I am so sorry for your loss. As we all know, there was only one Benjamin. He was the best dog, partly though, because you two were the best owners. It was such a touching bond you shared with one incredible animal. I hope you two are planning some time away, I'm sure Benjamin would be happy to know you are living and enjoying life! Thank you for keeping in touch. Benjamin will never be forgotten.

Allison

—

Malcolm, my heart goes out to you. Benjamin couldn't have had a better home, better parents, and better love and care. You will always have that as a source of comfort and eventually resolve, notwithstanding the cherished memories.

Thinking of you,

Janice

—

Dear Malcolm and Helen,

I got a shiver when I saw the subject of your message. I had a feeling what you were going to say...

The only time I had the pleasure of meeting Benjamin, I could tell what a special dog he was.

You are in my thoughts.

Hugs

Skee

—

Hi Malcolm and Helen,

I am so sorry to hear about your Benjamin. It is hard to imagine life without our beloved pet, as you say they enrich our lives.

Take care.

Nancy

—

Thank you for your wonderful hospitality today despite all the sadness, but the fact that so many people care has to be of some comfort in your tragic loss.

It is not given to everyone to be so loved as Benji was as well as yourselves.

Remember, I am just a floor away, and if you need a comfort of any kind, I am here.

Love Always

Pauline XX

—

Hi Malcolm,

I was very sorry to hear of Benjamin's passing. My most heartfelt condolences to you and Helen for your loss.

Paul

—

Just 20 minutes ago, after a 2 1/2 month daily battle, BELL returned my e-mail which it had taken away at the end of April. I just now retrieved your message. I am beyond saddened to get your news.

He was all you say and more. I have missed the idea of him for a long time. I, too, will never forget him. He was wonderfully special.
N.

—

Helen and Malcolm,

It was so good that Benjamin was at home with the two people who loved him as much as you two do. He was a wonderful dog and everyone in your building and people in my building who knew him all say that. When I was sitting with him in the lobby everyone knew him and said loving things about Ben. Today I had a couple here asked me about Benjamin, and when I told them about his passing they said he had a wonderful life with you, and "they must be devastated" knowing how much you both loved him.

I think about Benjamin every day and miss him. Being with him was a pleasure, and I was amazed at how well he handled all he was going through. It was always so nice to see both your reactions when you saw him and his getting up and running to you, snuggling — pure love all around. You were wonderful parents to him and he knew it. I know he brought you so much happiness and you'll always have all the memories. He's at peace now.

I really feel for both of you, the heartbreak and pain is so fresh and no one is ever ready for a pet's passing. I'm so sorry.

If I can help in any way, please call and I'll be a friend.
Take care,
Barbara

—

Hi Malcolm,

I've been away (and on vacation currently) but wanted to respond and tell you how sorry I am that you lost Benjamin. From personal experience, I know very well how much a part of the "family" man's best friend is.
Take care,
Bill

—

Dear Helen & Malcolm,

We got your beautiful and moving card about your dear boy Benjamin. No-one could have said it more eloquently than you did. Benjamin will be missed and continue to be loved by us too. I have misplaced the telephone number you gave to me in your phone message. If you get this email, please respond with that number or give me a call, when you feel up to it.

Love and warmest thoughts about Benjamin,

Joe, Jeff and Lucy

—

Benji was part of the landscape.

Harry

—

Hi Helen and Malcolm,

Thank you for the card with a beautiful picture of Benjamin on the front. All the notes are wonderful also — because Benjamin was everything you said. I have the card in my living room and will keep it and everything that I remember about Ben.

I hope that the pain is easing a little and know that you have many, many great memories of Benjamin that will always be with you.

Take care,

Barbara

—

Dear Malcolm and Helen,

It was so considerate and very wonderful of you to send the memorial card for Benji. We truly appreciate the great loss you have experienced and are thankful for allowing us to share in your grief. Benji was one of a kind and his photograph says everything. He was amazing and so human-like in all respects. The world would be a much better place if we were to have the same qualities and attributes that Benji displayed on a daily basis.

132

We have not seen you in the neighbourhood recently and trust all is well.

Keep in touch, with kindest and warmest regards,
Brian and Colette

—

OMG, I'm so so very sorry. I can't find the words right now. Will try calling you after work or this weekend if that's better for you.
Diane

—

Dear Malcolm and Helen,

I am deeply sorry for your loss. Benjamin was a very special doggie. I know you are both hurting very much from the pain of losing him. He had a wonderful life with you both and he will always be remembered, he will always be in your hearts. I lost my pets six years ago and everyday I remember how much love and joy they gave me. Our lives are truly enriched by our pets and their unconditional love. Time will heal your pain and you will always have your memories of your wonderful Benji. Thank you for the opportunity of doggie sitting Benji and spending time with him. He was and always will be a truly unique and wonderful doggie.

Jennifer

—

Dear Helen & Malcolm,

Yvonne and Pierre have made a donation to rescue a dog in honour of your beautiful boy Benjamin.

Enclosed is a Project Jessie Rescue package.

From Yvonne, Pierre, Jasper, Archer
Sincerely,
Sandra

—

Dear Malcolm & Helen,

We share your sorrow but pray that the good memories of Benjamin help carry you during this difficult period.

Love Diane and Keith

———

Dear Malcolm & Helen,

We are so sorry to hear that sad news and feel your pain. The only consolation is to think that Benjamin is no longer suffering anymore.

François & Gary

———

Dear Helen & Malcolm,

We were so sorry to learn of Benji's passing recently. He was so lovely and always enjoyed his walks with you. We loved seeing you together.

Know we are thinking of you…

Fondly,

Heather and Robin

———

Dear Helen & Malcolm,

Your card was so lovely & touching it took my breath away. I think a little of the spirit of Benjamin is in all of us.

We loved him & think the world of you.

Best wishes,

Wendy

———

These sentiments were expressed on a card from the wonderful staff at Pet Valu:

★ ★ ★

Helen & Malcolm,

I will miss Benjamin. You took such good care of him & he was loved so much. So sorry.

Lou
Kitty CAT Rescue

★ ★ ★

Thinking of you during this difficult time.
Amanda

★ ★ ★

Helen & Malcolm:
Condolences on the loss of sweet Benjamin. A wonderful dog.
Sue
Volunteer
Kitty CAT Rescue

★ ★ ★

So sorry for your loss.
Thinking of Benji…
– Daniel

★ ★ ★

Sorry for your loss
Justin

★ ★ ★

Sorry for your loss.
Teresa

———

Helen and Malcolm,

We're so sorry to hear of Benjamin's passing. He was such a sweet, kind dog, and was always so patient with Zoe. Please let us know when your book is published, and let us know if you need <u>anything</u>. Losing a friend like Benjamin is extremely tough.

Much love,

Jackie, Darren & Zoe 🐾

———

Dear Helen & Malcolm:

Sonny & I are so saddened by your beloved Benjamin's passing.

He was a dear sweet boy, and, know he will be missed by all of us, who knew and loved him over the years.

Benjamin had a blessed life with the two of you, and although you are devastated by his passing, I hope you find some comfort in knowing not only what he meant to you, but also what you meant to him. You are an inspiration to everyone who is lucky enough to know you.

Sonny & Tyrral & Ralph

—

Dear Helen and Malcolm.

Ricardo told me of Benjamin's death. I was so sorry to hear this. We always hope treatment would be successful.

Talley and I will miss seeing Benjamin in the lobby and outside. He was such a gentle dog and always a pleasure to meet.

You are both in my thoughts at this time.

Noreen

—

Dear Helen & Malcolm,

Our thoughts and prayers are with you as you mourn the loss of Benjamin.

Ray, Val & Dolce

—

Dear Helen & Malcolm

You are both in my heart over your loss of Benjamin.

I wish you the fondest memories of your dear, sweet companion.

He was our friend and mascot here at 33 Delisle.

I'll never forget his wirey coat, button nose and gorgeous big brown eyes.

Much love to you in your grief.

Fondly,

Ann

—

Dear Malcolm + Helen:

I was so sorry to hear about the passing of Ben. He was an institution here and the mascot for 33 Delisle.

He was the only dog in the building with whom I identified and whose name I always remembered!

My dog, Coco, died three years ago, and I too know what it means to lose a "member of the family".

I am enclosing two articles which I hope might give you some solace in your grief. I would also like you to know that a memorial donation is being sent to the Pet Trust at Guelph Vet. College in Ben's name.

You have all my sympathy and anything I can do to help you!

Mary Ann

—

Dear Malcolm & Helen, we were very saddened to learn of Benjamin's passing.

In life, the best walks are always too brief.

We are so sorry for your loss.

Al & Maureen

—

In this difficult time I only pray that God keep him in peace & rest his soul your so loving boy.

He was, is, & will be in our hearts always.

Andy and Family

—

May you find comfort in the warm embrace of family and friends

If there is anything you need please call us 24/7.

We all miss him!

Love and hugs

Wendy & Nancy

—

Dearest Helen & Malcolm,
So sad to learn of Benji's passing.
He was so very special not only to you but to all of us at 33 – he was such a very special "person" loved by us all.
Love Pauline xx

—

This must be so hard for you, but know that you gave him a wonderful and happy life.
My heart goes out to you both.
Peter

—

The following are from the staff in our building.

★ ★ ★

Dear Mr. Bernstein & Ms. Brent,
Our thoughts and sympathies are with you through this rough patch.
We dearly miss Benjamin,
Sincerely,
33 Delisle Staff
Marilyn

★ ★ ★

I am so sorry for you loss. Benjamin will be deeply missed.
Sincerely, Andre

★ ★ ★

We always miss him.
Andy

★ ★ ★

I will miss my favourite person in the hallway,
Sincerely sad.
Symmonetta

★ ★ ★

I still feel Benji in my arms. We lost one of our family members.
He will live in our memory forever.
Pirahl

★ ★ ★

I am so sorry for your loss, a part of 33 Delisle has left us. Benjiboo
is in a better place.
Ricardo

★ ★ ★

We will miss him dearly. So sorry for your loss.
Jennifer

★ ★ ★

With sympathy.
Kevin

—

Dear Helen & Malcolm,
My sincerest condolences on Benji's passing. My thoughts are
with you during this difficult time.
Love, Warren

—

Dear Helen & Malcolm,
Benjamin was a caring, loyal, kind Best Friend.

Thinking of you both — sharing your sense of loss and also fulfillment at the joyous years you had together. Benjamin's unique spirit will always live on.

Love,

Geoff, Joe, Lucy 🐾

———

To Helen and Malcolm.

Words alone cannot express our sadness surrounding Benjamin's passing. Our hearts go out to you.

Your memories of him will last forever, and your love for him and his for you will never fade.

We have made a donation to The Toronto Humane Society in Benjamin's memory.

Kind regards

Eric & Garrian

———

Dear Helen & Malcolm,

I have been out of town for a week & just learned that your 'Ben' has passed on.

I am so very sorry for you both. We will all miss Ben!

Sincerely,

Josephine

———

Dear Helen & Malcolm,

Many thoughts and prayers are with you at this sad time.

Sorry for your loss.

Irene & Walter

———

With each new day may peace find a place in your heart.

Sharing in your sorrow.

Benjamin was the greatest, sweetest dog.

Barbara

—

Hi Malcolm and Helen
The gifts your dog gave you — happiness, companionship, unconditional love — those will never leave you.
They are yours to treasure forever.
Benji will always be remembered.
With Sympathy,
Chris and Sherry

—

Helen & Malcolm,
With sympathies on the loss of Benjamin.
Sincerely,
Lynne

—

Dear Malcolm
We were both so sorry to hear about the loss of your beautiful Benjamin.
Truly, animals know and teach us the true meaning of the word 'Love' but no-one else. We know the loss is devastating and hope that your grief has helped a little by knowing that he could not possibly have had a better, or more loving hands 'pass him through the door'.
Now there is no more pain or suffering — only love and treasured memories.
We know how hard the days ahead may be — for who else follows us from room to room, always eager to see us?
But hold to your heart that there never was a better-loved doggie than your 'Benji'.
Love from Alison & Peter

—

Malcolm & Helen.

My thoughts and prayers are with you.
Sharon

—

My dearest Malcolm and Helen,
Please accept this note as support for you as you face this deep loss. As a fellow animal owner, I understand the joy and sadness that our furry creatures bring — joy when alive — sadness in death. I am sure that every living day of Benji's life was full of love and happiness.
Rita

—

Faithful friendship,
Warm memories,
Unconditional love –
Wonderful gifts
From a loving pet.
How lucky you were
To have such a good friend…
How sad you must be
To say good-bye.
In sympathy
Susan

—

Dear Helen
I am so very sorry to hear the news about Benjamin. I am glad that I got to see him yesterday one last time. He was so adorable and I know you will miss him.
Take care and enjoy your time in Montreal.
Kimberly

—

Dear Malcolm & Helen,

I was so saddened to hear of Benjamin's passing. I hope you have many fond memories to keep his spirit alive.

Thinking of you.

Brad

—

Dearest Helen & Malcolm,

There are no words to say for the loss of your beautiful baby Benjamin.

"When tomorrow starts without me

Don't think we are far apart

For every time you think of me

I am right here inside your heart."

With deepest sympathy,

All our love,

Max, Elaine, Sushi & Persia XOXOXOXO

If there is anything you need or I can do for you. Just let me know. We love you both very much. Our hearts & thoughts are with you.

—

The following letter was received from the University of Guelph, Ontario Veterinary College Pet Trust Fund for donations made in Benjamin's memory by these friends and family Dale; Diane and Keith; Mary Ann; Jeff, Nina and Maddy.

★ ★ ★

Dear Helen and Malcolm,

We were truly sorry to learn of the passing of your beloved dog, Benjamin. In recognition of your loving relationship with Benjamin, a monetary donation has been made to the Ontario Veterinary College (OVC) Pet Trust. Pet Trust honours the amazing relationship between pets, people and the veterinary caregivers. This kind gift will support learning and lead to advances in our knowledge to improve the health of our companions. I think you will agree that this is a wonderful tribute to your special friend. You can find out more about the OVC Pet Trust at www.pettrust.ca

As veterinarians and animal lovers, we understand how painful losing a pet can be. We hope that you derive comfort from knowing that this gift in memory of Benjamin will help move veterinary medicine forward. Our thoughts are with you at this difficult time.

Sincerely,

Dr. Gordon Kirby, DVM, MSc, PhD.

Associate Dean, Research and Innovation

—

This letter was received from the Farley Foundation.

★ ★ ★

Dear Mr. Bernstein.

It was my pleasure to inform you that a donation to the Farley Foundation was kindly made in memory of Benjamin by your babysitter, Kasey, who would like to express her personal sympathy for your loss. Benjamin was one of a kind and you can always take solace in knowing that you rescued him, and gave him the best life possible.

My thoughts are with you.

The Farley Foundation assists people in need in subsidizing the costs of veterinary care for the pets that mean the world to them.

Sincerely,

Douglas Raven

Executive Director

—

The following donations were made by each of Rosalie, Lynne, and Fern to The Toronto Humane Society

★ ★ ★

A special donation has been made in loving memory of Benjamin supporting the animals at The Toronto Humane Society.

This gift will truly make a difference in the lives of the animals that come through our doors.

★ ★ ★

These words in Fern's card:

★ ★ ★

In loving memory of Benjamin, who will be missed and joyfully celebrated. May memories of your sweet boy be of comfort to you and Helen.
Much love, Fern

★ ★ ★

A donation has been made in memory of Benjamin to the Ontario Society of the Prevention of Cruelty to Animals.

May you treasure your memories of Benjamin's unconditional love, loyalty and friendship
Claudette and Holger

CPSIA information can be obtained
at www.ICGtesting.com
Printed in the USA
LVHW02s1110300118
564501LV00001B/22/P